A BRAND-NEW YEAR—
A PROMISING NEW START

With expert readings and forecasts, you can chart a course to romance, adventure, good health, or career opportunities while gaining valuable insight into yourself and others. Offering a daily outlook for 18 full months, this fascinating guide shows you:

* The important dates in your life
* What to expect from an astrological reading
* How the stars can help you stay healthy and fit
  And more!

Let this sound advice guide you through a year of heavenly possibilities—for today and for every day of 2014!

SYDNEY OMARR'S® DAY-BY-DAY
ASTROLOGICAL GUIDE FOR

ARIES—March 21–April 19
TAURUS—April 20–May 20
GEMINI—May 21–June 20
CANCER—June 21–July 22
LEO—July 23–August 22
VIRGO—August 23–September 22
LIBRA—September 23–October 22
SCORPIO—October 23–November 21
SAGITTARIUS—November 22–December 21
CAPRICORN—December 22–January 19
AQUARIUS—January 20–February 18
PISCES—February 19–March 20

IN 2014

SYDNEY OMARR'S®

DAY-BY-DAY ASTROLOGICAL GUIDE FOR

TAURUS

APRIL 20–MAY 20

2014

by Trish MacGregor
with Rob MacGregor

A SIGNET BOOK

SIGNET
Published by the Penguin Group
Penguin Group (USA) Inc., 375 Hudson Street,
New York, New York 10014, USA

USA / Canada / UK / Ireland / Australia / New Zealand / India / South Africa / China

Penguin Books Ltd., Registered Offices: 80 Strand, London WC2R 0RL, England
For more information about the Penguin Group visit penguin.com.

First published by Signet, an imprint of New American Library,
a division of Penguin Group (USA) Inc.

First Printing, June 2013

ISBN 978-0-451-41386-4

Printed in the United States of America
10 9 8 7 6 5 4 3 2 1

ALWAYS LEARNING   PEARSON

CONTENTS

CHAPTER 1

The New You

We branded 2012 the year of the paradigm shift, and since the world didn't end, 2013 became the year of transformation. Now here you are at the doorstep of 2014, and the person who steps through is the new you!

And who is this new you likely to be? For some clues, let's take a look at the transits of the outer planets this year. These planets exert the most influence over our daily lives because they take so long to move through a single sign. Pluto, for instance, entered Capricorn in 2008 and won't leave until early 2024. Neptune, which takes about fourteen years to move through a sign, entered Pisces in early February 2012 and will be there until late January 2026. Uranus entered Aries in March 2011 and leaves that sign in March 2019. So just these three planets exert a powerful influence over a number of years.

The next two planets that influence us over a period of time are Saturn, which takes two and a half years to transit a sign, and Jupiter, which usually takes about a year. Each of these planets is covered extensively in various parts of the book, and each one has its role in the formation of the new you in 2014.

In the next chapter we talk about what each of the planets represents, what signs they rule, and just about anything else you could ever want to know about them astrologically. In a later chapter historical perspectives are provided on the three slowest-moving planets. But this chapter let's take an in-depth look at the planet Uranus and how its energies will help define the new you.

Uranus

This planet symbolizes revolution, genius, rebellion, earthquakes, sudden, unexpected events and change, our individuality, inventions and discoveries, electricity, radio, TV, electronics, lightning. You get the idea. Its energy isn't the least bit subtle. It sweeps into our lives, stirs up mass movements, and knocks down the old to make way for the new.

On March 11, 2011, the day that Uranus entered Aries, there was a 9.0 earthquake near the east coast of Honshu, Japan. The quake triggered a twenty-three-foot tsunami that hammered Japan's coast and caused an explosion at the Fukushima nuclear plant and the subsequent worst nuclear disaster since Chernobyl twenty-five years ago.

Any country would be devastated by just one of these events. But to have all three within twenty-four hours resulted in some staggering statistics. According to an earthquake report issued by http://earthquake-report.com, about twenty thousand people are either dead or missing; more than a million buildings were destroyed, eighty thousand residents were evacuated from a twelve-mile radius around the plant, and the economic losses range from between $100 to $500 billion, most of it created within seventy minutes.

As of late 2011 the evacuees have still not been permitted to go home, and the authorities are still cooling down the plant. The environmental ministry in Japan says an area of 930 square mi is affected.

All of these events are right in line with the archetypal energy of Uranus transiting Aries, the warrior.

Other facets of this transit are revolution and rebellion. First there were the uprisings in the Arab world in late 2010 that swept three leaders out of power—the heads of Tunisia, Egypt, and Libya. Then in September 2011 came a grassroots protest: Occupy Wall Street. On September 17 about two thousand people congregated in downtown Manhattan and marched up Broadway. En route they stopped at Zuccotti Park and more than a hundred of the protesters stayed the night and set up an encampment.

The mainstream media ignored the protest at first. Then Keith Olbermann, on Current TV, started covering it, and suddenly so did everyone else. From the Occupy Web site: ". . . we kicked off a protest against bank bailouts, corporate greed, and the unchecked power of Wall Street in Washington." The movement rapidly gained global support, and by its one-month anniversary had spread to eighty-two countries.

It takes eighty-four years for Uranus to move through the zodiac. So let's take a trip down memory lane to the last time Uranus transited the sign of Aries. In mid-January 1928 Uranus entered Aries and remained there until late March 1935. Here are some of the events that occurred during this period:

- First air-conditioned office opens in the U.S. in San Antonio
- Scotch tape first marketed by 3M company
- First trans-Atlantic TV image received
- Amelia Earhart first woman to fly the Atlantic— as a passenger
- Alexander Fleming discovers penicillin
- Yo-yo introduced
- First regularly scheduled TV is broadcast three nights a week
- German airship *Graf Zeppelin* begins a round-the-world flight
- Stock market crash
- Salvador Dali's first one-man show
- Bingo invented
- Planet Pluto named
- Hostess Twinkies invented
- N.Y. Yankee Babe Ruth hits three consecutive homers
- First nudist colony opens
- First radar detection of planes
- *N.Y. World* reports disappearance of supreme court justice Joseph Crater
- N.Y.C. College offers first course in radio advertising
- A bloodless coup d'état in Brazil
- First *Dracula* movie released
- Empire State Building opens in N.Y.C.
- Al Capone is indicted on 5,000 counts of prohibition and perjury

- Babe Ruth hits his 600th home run
- Alka Seltzer goes on sale
- Jane Addams—first U.S. woman named corecipient of Nobel Peace Prize
- Martial law is declared in Honduras to stop revolt by banana workers fired by United Fruit
- El Salvador army kills four thousand protesting farmers
- First patent issued for a tree, to James Markham for a peach tree
- Amelia Earhart is first woman to fly solo across the Atlantic
- Yellow fever vaccine for humans announced
- U.S. federal gas tax enacted
- Earthquake kills seventy thousand in Kansu, China
- Hitler proclaims end of Marxism
- Bank holidays declared in six states to prevent run on banks
- F.D.R. inaugurated as thirty-second pres, pledges to pull U.S. out of Depression and says, "We have nothing to fear but fear itself."
- F.D.R. proclaims ten-day bank holiday
- Dachau, first concentration camp, completed
- First flight over Mount Everest
- Nazis stage public book burnings in Germany
- Loch Ness Monster is first reported
- German Secret State Police (Gestapo) established
- In London five hundred thousand march against anti-Semitism
- Alcatraz officially becomes a federal prison
- *Flash Gordon* comic strip debuts

- F.D.R. signs Home Owners Loan Act
- First Sugar Bowl and first Orange Bowl
- First canned beer is sold
- Monopoly is invented
- First Penguin book is published
- Four hundred thousand demonstrators against fascism in Madrid
- *Billboard* magazine publishes its first music Hit Parade
- The first stock car race is held in Daytona Beach, Florida
- *Gone With the Wind* by Margaret Mitchell is published
- Spanish Civil War begins; General Francisco Franco leads uprising
- King Edward VIII abdicates throne to marry Mrs. Wallis Simpson

This list represents just a small sampling of the thousands of events that occurred during Uranus' last transit of Aries. But as you read through this list you undoubtedly see a pattern—war, rebellion, uprisings, numerous discoveries and many "firsts," the rise of Hitler and Nazi Germany, natural disasters like earthquakes, the completion of engineering marvels like the Empire State Building and Hoover Dam, the precipitous drop of the stock market and the depression that followed.

Aries is not only the sign of the warrior, but of the entrepreneur, the trailblazer, the one who is so independent and forward thinking that he marches to a different drummer. Aries is fearless, a risk-taker, and like the *Star Trek* motto, goes where no man (or woman) has gone before. So when you combine Aries with the planet that symbolizes all the traits mentioned earlier, you have an intriguing MO for the emergence of the new you.

The new you will be emerging into a new planetary environment, so let's start there.

Innovations

Book publishing. Once the dust settles, the book publishing industry and retail bookstores in general will be vastly changed from the way they have existed for years. The emergence of the eBook, the Kindle, Nook, and other electronic reading devices is, as of this writing in early 2012, creating chaos. With the bankruptcy of Borders Books, Barnes & Noble is the only game left in town, the largest book retailer in the U.S., and they don't stock every book that is published. So what happens to a book when Barnes & Noble doesn't carry it? That depends.

If the book is an eBook that sells for a fraction of the price of a hardback book—$9.99 versus, say, $25 or $30—perhaps the lack of hardcover sales are compensated for because more people can afford to buy an eBook than a hardcover. A young woman in Minnesota wrote a romance novel that was rejected by major publishers, so she self-published the novel as an eBook, sold it for $2.99, and sold millions of copies. Within a year she paid a million cash for her first home.

So what might we expect this year? Perhaps the publishing and bookstore industry are learning that life is interconnected. Ebooks, after all, save trees. Saving trees helps the environment. Helping the environment aids the planet. So perhaps by the time this transit is finished ebooks will be the norm, and only libraries will carry print books.

Another possible repercussion is that more authors will self-publish in ebooks. With the advent of blogs and online software that makes building a Web site easier than a few years ago, there may come a time when authors charge for access to their blogs, where entire novels and books are written.

More social media. MySpace, Facebook, Twitter, LinkedIn, Google Friends ... before Uranus leaves Aries, expect more social media to surface. Uranus rules the Internet, so the Internet itself may evolve and change in important ways before the end of this transit.

Medical breakthroughs. During Uranus' last transit of Aries, the medical breakthroughs were significant: treatment for yellow fever, development of penicillin, anesthesia, insulin shock therapy, vitamin B3, and protonsil, the first sulphur drug, which was used to treat infections caused by streptococcus. So this time around we can expect other types of breakthroughs in medicine, health, and pharmacology. A cure for AIDS? Cancer? Heart disease?

Rebellion/revolution. More planetary changes are likely, and so is continued rebellion by the 99 percent. The us-versus-them mentality has brought about a wider gap between rich and poor, with the middle class fading rapidly. Groups of urban survivalists have sprung up, some of them extremists.

The U.S., with the most powerful military in the world (which also eats up the largest chunk of the federal budget), continues to police the rest of the planet, while pushing the needs of its own citizens into a dark hole labeled *later*.

The contentiousness of the political divide in the U.S. was glaringly obvious in the health care debate that raged in early 2011 and later that year in the debt crisis debates. These trends, unfortunately, may get worse before Uranus leaves Aries.

However, if we remember that Uranus' job is to shake up the status quo so that new paradigms, new ways of doing things, can be born, then we could see the birth of new political parties that emphasize peace over war. Perhaps we'll see a complete withdrawal of U.S. troops from the Mideast.

Politics. The warrior archetype is certainly prevalent these days in politics. As a new paradigm is being birthed, the old paradigm isn't dying an easy death.

The meltdown in 2008 resulted in massive bailouts to banks, the collapse of institutions, and billions of stimulus dollars poured into the economy. It was the Obama administration's equivalent of F.D.R.'s New Deal, passed during his first term in response to the Great Depression. During this period Social Security was implemented.

As Uranus continues its transit through Aries, we may see the implementation of new social or economic programs that aid people rather than banks and corporations. It's doubtful we'll see any true universal health coverage, at least not if the past is any indication. But *if* a visionary was swept into the White House in 2016, *if* the corporate greed has been overturned, *if* Wall Street is regulated and the entire banking system overhauled, then maybe. But it's a lot of *if*s.

Discoveries. Numerous discoveries and inventions came about during Uranus's last pass through Aries. This transit could produce the twenty-first–century equivalents in technology, television, the Internet, health and medicine, engineering, movies, earthquake detection, music, ebooks, alternative fuels.

World records. During Uranus' last transit of Aries many "firsts" occurred, and world records were set. This time around we could see more of the same—in space flight, cars that run on alternative fuels, high-speed trains, athletics, even the ways our homes and office buildings are powered. The world may go green more quickly than we can imagine.

With Uranus, we either embrace change—or it's forced upon us. So let's take a look at how each of us can embrace the change Uranus is ushering into our personal lives.

Aries ♈

Cardinal Fire Sign

The new you is likely to be an improved version of the old you. The things you disliked about yourself a few years ago will fall away. Maybe a belief system you clung to a few years back was no longer serving your best interests and has now shattered, and you're casting about for new beliefs, new ways of being. Or perhaps a significant relationship has fallen apart. Or you lost your job. In whatever area your life was sterile and routine, Uranus has shaken things up.

As an Aries, you're probably well aware of where your life is stale and routine and do your best to turn it around. That means you're ahead of the game, and the Uranus transit through your sign will be exciting. But in the event you're the rare Aries who doesn't mind routine, this transit will be jarring, and the new you will emerge from the shock. Uranus has been in Aries for about three years now, so you should have a fairly clear idea how the transit is affecting you.

The best way for you to navigate this transit is to do what you do naturally: maintain a sense of adventure about life; be passionate in all that you undertake; keep your steady focus, don't hesitate to explore. In addition treat others the way you like to be treated. In love relationships strive to be more cooperative, to see things the way your partner does. In your career, with your creative work, complete what you start.

Unusual ideas and idiosyncratic individuals are part of this transit package. You won't be bored, but be careful that life doesn't become just one adrenaline high after the other. Welcome change, embrace it, even if it's thrust on you.

Taurus ♉

Fixed Earth Sign

Unless you have some planets in fire signs, you probably won't like this transit very much. It jars your grounded, Taurean sensibilities. However, because you're the most stubborn, resilient, and resolute sign in the zodiac, you come through it intact, with a new you to show to the world.

The new you in 2014 may be less stubborn, for one thing. The Uranus transit, after all, occurs in your solar twelfth house, so a lot of *stuff* is being stirred up in your unconscious. You may discover power you have disowned over the years and take it back. Or you may discover your dreams are filled with insights and information that aid you. Ideas that come to you during this transit are likely to be unusual, and it will be up to that grounded side of your personality to translate them into something useful.

As a fixed earth sign, you like things in your life to be orderly, practical, even predictable. You're slow to change your opinions and beliefs. *Stability* is your middle name. Since this transit occurs in your solar twelfth house, Uranus shakes up your world from the inside out. Your greatest strength during this period is to tackle one issue at a time and deal with it the way you do everything else in your life—carefully, thoroughly, meticulously.

The new you who emerges this year is the Taurus who has tackled these issues and reclaimed personal power and is ready to embrace everything that comes your way.

Gemini ♊

Mutable Air Sign

The new you who emerges in 2014 is likely to be more focused, ready to implement all the unusual ideas that are flowing through you. The way you implement these ideas, of course, is through your communication skills and by using your flexibility to quickly adapt to new situations.

Uranus forms a beneficial angle to your sun during

this transit, which enhances your innate abilities and attracts unusual people, excitement, and abrupt, positive change. It occurs in your solar eleventh house of friends, wishes, and dreams. The new you is apt to be more involved in a group—a theater group, writing, bridge, esoteric—that supports your interests and passions. In some way this group helps you to achieve your wishes and dreams.

New opportunities should surface for self-expression. If you've always had a secret yearning to write a novel or screenplay, for example, this transit helps you to do it. If you're an amateur photographer, you may have an opportunity to become a professional. The transit will free you from limiting circumstances—a relationship that no longer works, a job that has grown stale and predictable, a career that no longer feels right. Your comfortable ruts will become history.

Cancer ♋
Cardinal Water Sign

In 2014 the new you is a career-oriented individual. The Uranus transit through Aries forms a challenging angle to your sun and occurs in your tenth house of career, so you've probably experienced or are experiencing radical, abrupt professional changes. Your job, for example, could be outsourced. Or you get a new boss whom you don't like. Or you have to take a cut in pay. Whatever the curve ball that Uranus in Aries throws your way, Cancer, regard it as an opportunity, and watch the new you begin to take shape.

The new you will be able to draw steadily upon the

vast reservoir of your intuition, will gain immeasurably from insights and information gleaned from your dreams, and will be readily able to put these insights to work.

The lens through which you see the world is personal, subjective, emotional. Your nurturing and intuitive abilities are your greatest strengths and will serve the new you even better than they served the former you! You eagerly seek out the new and different and embrace change.

Leo ♌

Fixed Fire Sign

The new you who emerges from this transit will have vastly improved skills and talents and less ego. Uranus forms a beneficial angle to your sun during this transit and bolsters all the qualities for which you're known and loved—your warmth, compassion, flair for drama, and ability to make friends with just about anyone.

The sudden, exciting changes that are brought about prompt you to try new forms of self-expression. Your creative drive soars. The stimulating people you encounter during this transit, individuals who may be geniuses in their fields, may prove helpful to you in some way. There could be romance and love with this transit too, Leo. So many intriguing individuals are entering your life now that you'll have your pick!

The new you may undertake a spiritual quest of some kind and travel abroad in search of esoteric knowledge. Or you may go to college, grad school, or law school. You will make time to keep yourself fit and healthy through a regular fitness regimen.

Virgo ♍
Mutable Earth Sign

This transit forms a challenging angle to your sun sign and is shaking up those areas that have become routine in your life. The new you who emerges this year will still be a perfectionist who is precise and detailed oriented, but no longer to the point of obsession.

The transit occurs in your solar eighth house—shared resources. Since the eighth house represents joint resources, your partner's income may rise or fall suddenly or unexpectedly. You could inherit money. It's an excellent time to get out of debt. In fact, debt may be another limitation that you find intolerable. The new you will probably be more frugal, paying for things in cash.

Any new romance that comes your way could be highly sexual and have a deeply intuitive component to it.

Libra ♎
Cardinal Air Sign

The new you who emerges in 2014 will still possess all the wonderful qualities that make you the person so many people love. You will still be able to put yourself in someone else's shoes and see the world through the eyes of another. But you aren't as likely to bend over backward to please other people, and finding peace and harmony won't be as difficult as it may have been in the past.

The new you will reach out to people more readily. The social grace with which you do this will enable you to win over the opposition every time. This transit occurs in your solar seventh house of partnerships. Both romantic and business partnerships could be challenged during this transit, but you ride the tide, whatever it is, and learn from the experiences. When sudden, unexpected events bring about the beginning and end of partnerships, you stand up for who you are and what you really believe, and in doing so you break free of restrictions that have become unbearable.

This transit may seem harsh at times. It appears that stuff is happening *to* you, that the universe is ganging up against you. But what's actually happening is that energies you have repressed over the years are now scrambling for release. Any relationship that ends under this transit—through death or otherwise—does so because it has served its purpose. Relationships that begin during this transit are apt to be exciting, different in some way, and stimulating mentally, emotionally, and spiritually.

Go with the flow, Libra. That's the new you.

Scorpio ♏

Fixed Water Sign

The new you who emerges in 2014 is influenced by several factors—Uranus in Aries, certainly, but also by

Saturn transiting your sign, something we'll talk about in a later chapter. This new you will be more intuitive and less stubborn and perhaps less secretive as well. You will continue to delve deeply for answers, but in a less obsessive way. You won't be doing it with a feeling that it must be done immediately. Tomorrow or next week will work fine too.

This transit is about freedom—from restrictions and limitations in any area of your life that prevent you from evolving creatively, spiritually, or emotionally. As a fixed water sign, you probably don't like change any more than your fixed-sign brothers— Taurus, Leo, and Aquarius. But change you must. It's easier if you can learn to embrace change rather than resist it so that change isn't thrust on you, and that's what the new you achieves!

Since this transit occurs in your solar sixth house, the area most likely to be impacted is your daily work routine and health. The possible scenarios depend on how rigid, routine, or boring your daily work is; whether you stick to this work primarily because it's comfortable; and whether or not you enjoy what you're doing. The health aspect depends on how well you take care of yourself and your beliefs about health. In other words, if you believe that people get colds every winter, you probably will get a cold every winter. So take inventory of your beliefs, Scorpio. The new, emerging you has a clear handle on his or her beliefs.

Sagittarius ♐
Mutable Fire Sign

The new you who emerges from this Uranus transit, Sagittarius, is as exciting and adventurous as always, but with some important changes. You're now ready to actually be in a romantic partnership, to communicate honestly with your partner, to give for the joy of giving. It's likely that romantic relationships begin and end suddenly and your creativity is taking you in new directions. The new you is fine with whatever is happening. You eagerly embrace the changes in your life.

With Uranus in Aries forming a beneficial angle to your sun, you're able to become who you really are; it's much easier to reshape your personality. Your creative self-expression shines forth, and new venues for creativity open up. You may find yourself involved in creative projects that are totally different from anything you've done before, that prompt you to stretch your creativity in new ways.

If you're a Sadge who enjoys travel—and you probably are, many of your sign do—you'll be doing more of it during this transit. In fact, abundant foreign travel may be an intricate part of the new you.

Capricorn ♑
Cardinal Earth Sign

The new you who emerges in 2014 will be just as focused as you usually are, but with less of an obsessive edge. You're not obsessive the way a Scorpio is, for instance, but there can be an intensity about your focus that doesn't serve your best interests. Your ability to plow through any obstacle you encounter will enable you to break free of any limitations and restrictions that are either self-imposed or imposed on you by others. The new you will have better methods for doing this.

The transit occurs in your solar fourth house—your domestic environment—so let's take a look at some possible scenarios:

Your parents move in with you.

Your employer is relocating, and if you want to keep your job, you have to move too.

Your partner or spouse is laid off at work, and you have to sell your home and move to a smaller place.

Your parents get divorced, and you have to relocate.

The fourth house represents the foundation of your life, the most intimate and personal part of who you are. For most of us, changes in this area can be deeply unsettling. Any part of this area that has grown stale, rigid, or routine will be affected. But if your home life is vibrant and exciting, then it won't be impacted.

The new you will strive to be more flexible and will be better equipped to go with the flow emotionally, creatively, and spiritually.

Aquarius ≈
Fixed Air Sign

The new you who emerges this year will be edgier and more idiosyncratic, with more unusual ideas. The Uranus transit through Aries forms a beneficial angle to your sun and occurs in your solar third house, which represents communication, your conscious mind, neighborhood and neighbors, siblings, daily life, and travel. This area is where you're apt to experience all the excitement of this transit—and the place from which the new you emerges.

The new you is excited by the exploration of consciousness and how it molds and shapes our perceptions, and how, in fact, it may attract the kinds of experiences we have. During this transit your consciousness is expanding, leaping outward, seeking new ideas, and exploring different belief systems and lifestyles. You may move quite suddenly and unexpectedly, but it turns out to be beneficial for you. You may undertake creative projects that are outside your usual talents and abilities and discover a new facet of your personality. This period is all about trying the new and unexplored, adventures in consciousness and communication.

The new you knows it's the ideal time to start a blog, build a Web site, or write a novel or book and gets involved with community activities. Uranus, the planet that rules your sign, won't disappoint you during this transit.

Pisces ♓

Mutable Water Sign

The new you who emerges this year is just as imaginative and intuitive as always but less conflicted, so it's easier for you to make decisions. Like your mutable siblings—Gemini, Virgo, and Sagittarius—you don't have any problem with change. But because this transit occurs in a fire sign, Aries, your solar second house of finances, this is the area where the new you is likely to emerge.

The new you will insist on working in a profession or career that is in line with your deeper beliefs and ideals. The new you will follow intuitive leads, network with others of like mind, and strive to turn any challenge into a blessing. You'll understand that nothing is too wild to try, too *out there* to consider. The new you will understand the wisdom of financial prudence, will pay cash for everything, and probably cut up the credit cards too.

CHAPTER 2

Astrological Basics

On the day you were born, what was the weather like? If you were born at night, had the moon already risen? Was it full or the shape of a Cheshire cat's grin? Was the delivery ward quiet or bustling with activity? Unless your mom or dad has a very good memory, you'll probably never know the full details. But there's one thing you can know for sure: on the day you were born the sun was located in a particular zone of the zodiac, an imaginary 360-degree belt that circles the earth. The belt is divided into twelve 30-degree portions called signs.

If you were born between July 23 and August 22, the sun was passing through the sign of Leo, so we say that your sun sign is Leo. Each of the twelve signs has distinct attributes and characteristics. Leos, for instance, love being the center of attention. They're warm, compassionate people with a flair for the dramatic. Virgos, born between August 23 and September 22, are perfectionists with discriminating intellects and a genius for details. Capricorns, born between

December 22 and January 19, are the worker bees of the zodiac, serious minded, ambitious, industrious.

How Signs Are Classified

As you probably gathered from the first chapter, the twelve signs are categorized according to element and quality or modality. The first category, element, reads like a basic science lesson—fire, earth, air, and water—and describes the general physical characteristics of the signs.

Fire signs—Aries, Leo, Sagittarius—are warm, dynamic individuals who are always passionate about what they do.

Earth signs—Taurus, Virgo, Capricorn—are the builders of the zodiac, practical and efficient, grounded in everything they do.

Air signs—Gemini, Libra, Aquarius—are people who live mostly in the world of ideas. They are terrific communicators.

Water signs—Cancer, Scorpio, Pisces—live through their emotions, imaginations, and intuitions.

The second category describes how each sign operates in the physical world, how adaptable it is to circumstances:

Cardinal signs—Aries, Cancer, Libra, Capricorn—are initiators. These people are active, impatient, restless. They're great at starting things, but unless a project or a relationship holds their attention, they lose interest and may not finish what they start.

Fixed signs—Taurus, Leo, Scorpio, Aquarius—are deliberate, controlled, resolute. These individuals tend to move more slowly than cardinal signs, are often stubborn, and resist change. They seek roots and stability and are always in the game for the long haul. They aren't quitters.

Mutable signs — Gemini, Virgo, Sagittarius, Pisces — are adaptable. These people are flexible, changeable, communicative. They don't get locked into rigid patterns or belief systems.

TABLE 1 SUN SIGNS

Sign	Date	Element	Quality
Aries ♈	March 21–April 19	Fire	Cardinal
Taurus ♉	April 20–May 20	Earth	Fixed
Gemini ♊	May 21–June 21	Air	Mutable
Cancer ♋	June 22–July 22	Water	Cardinal
Leo ♌	July 23–August 22	Fire	Fixed
Virgo ♍	August 23–September 22	Earth	Mutable
Libra ♎	September 23–October 22	Air	Cardinal
Scorpio ♏	October 23–November 21	Water	Fixed
Sagittarius ♐	November 22–December 21	Fire	Mutable
Capricorn ♑	December 22–January 19	Earth	Cardinal
Aquarius ♒	January 20–February 18	Air	Fixed
Pisces ♓	February 19–March 20	Water	Mutable

The Planets

The planets in astrology are the players who make things happen. They're the characters in the story of your life. This story always begins with the sun, the giver of life.

Your sun sign describes your self-expression, your primal energy, the essence of who you are. It's the archetypal pattern of your Self. When you know another person's sun sign, you already have a great deal of information about that person. Let's say you're a Taurus who has just started dating a Gemini. How compatible are you?

On the surface, it wouldn't seem that you have much in common. Taurus is a fixed earth sign; Gemini is a mutable air sign. Taurus is persistent, stubborn, practical, a cultivator as opposed to an initiator. Gemini is a chameleon, a communicator, social, with a mind as quick as lightning. Taurus is ruled by Venus, which governs the arts, money, beauty, love, and romance, and Gemini is ruled by Mercury, which governs communication and travel. There doesn't seem to be much common ground. But before we write off this combination, let's look a little deeper.

Suppose the Taurus has Mercury in Gemini, and suppose the Gemini has Venus in Taurus? This would mean that the Taurus and Gemini each have their rulers in the other person's sign. They probably communicate well and enjoy travel and books (Mercury) and would see eye to eye on romance, art, and music (Venus). They might get along so well, in fact, that they collaborate on creative projects.

Each of us is also influenced by the other nine planets (the sun and moon are treated like planets in astrology) and the signs they were transiting when you were born. Suppose our Taurus and Gemini have the same moon sign? The moon rules our inner needs, emotions and intuition, and all that makes us feel secure within ourselves. Quite often compatible moon signs can overcome even the most glaring difference in sun signs because the two people share similar emotions.

In the sections on predictions your sun sign always takes center stage, and every prediction is based on the movement of the transiting planets in relation to your sun sign. Let's say you're a Sagittarius. Between November 16 and December 11 this year Venus will be transiting your sign. What's this mean for you? Well, since Venus rules—among other things—romance, you can expect your love life to pick up significantly during these weeks. Other people will find you attractive and be more open to your ideas, and you'll radiate a certain charisma. Your creative endeavors will move full steam ahead.

Table 2 provides an overview of the planets and the signs that they rule. Keep in mind that the moon is the swiftest-moving planet, changing signs about every two and a half days, and that Pluto is the snail of the zodiac, taking as long as thirty years to transit a single sign. Although the faster-moving planets—the moon, Mercury, Venus, and Mars—have an impact on our lives, it's the slow pokes—Uranus, Neptune, and Pluto—that bring about the most profound influence and change. Jupiter and Saturn fall between the others in terms of speed. This year Jupiter spends the first six months in Cancer, then enters Leo on July 16 and doesn't leave that sign until August 11, 2015.

In the section on predictions the most frequent references are to the transits of Mercury, Venus, and Mars and the movements of the transiting moon.

Now glance through Table 2. When a sign is in parentheses, it means the planet corules that sign. This assignation dates back to when we thought there were only seven planets in the solar system. But since there were still twelve signs, some of the planets had to do double duty!

TABLE 2 THE PLANETS

Planet	Rules	Attributes of Planet
Sun ☉	Leo	Self-expression, primal energy, creative ability, ego, individuality
Moon ☽	Cancer	Emotions, intuition, mother or wife, security
Mercury ☿	Gemini, Virgo	Intellect, mental acuity, communication, logic, reasoning, travel, contracts
Venus ♀	Taurus, Libra	Love, romance, beauty, artistic instincts, the arts, music, material and financial resources
Mars ♂	Aries (Scorpio)	Physical and sexual energy, aggression, drive
Jupiter ♃	Sagittarius (Pisces)	Luck, expansion, success, prosperity, growth, creativity, spiritual interests, higher education, law
Saturn ♄	Capricorn (Aquarius)	Laws of physical universe, discipline, responsibility, structure, karma, authority
Uranus ♅	Aquarius	Individuality, genius, eccentricity, originality, science, revolution

Planet	Rules	Attributes of Planet
Neptune ♆	Pisces	Visionary self, illusions, what's hidden, psychic ability, dissolution of ego boundaries, spiritual insights, dreams
Pluto ♀ ♇	Scorpio	The darker side, death, sex, regeneration, rebirth, profound and permanent change, transformation

Houses and Rising Signs

In the instant you drew your first breath, one of the signs of the zodiac was just passing over the eastern horizon. Astrologers refer to this as the rising sign or ascendant. It's what makes your horoscope unique. Think of your ascendant as the front door of your horoscope, the place where you enter into this life and begin your journey.

Your ascendant is based on the exact moment of your birth, and the other signs follow counterclockwise. If you have Taurus rising, for example, that is the cusp of your first house. The cusp of the second would be Gemini, of the third Cancer, and so on around the horoscope circle in a counterclockwise direction. Each house governs a particular area of life, which is outlined below.

The best way to find out your rising sign is to have your horoscope drawn up by an astrologer. For those of you with access to the Internet, though, there are several sites that provide free birth horoscopes: www

.astro.com and www.cafeastrology.com are two good ones.

In a horoscope the ascendant (cusp of the first house), IC (cusp of the fourth house), descendant (cusp of the seventh house) and MC (cusp of the tenth house) are considered to be the most critical angles. Any planets that fall close to these angles are extremely important in the overall astrological picture of who you are. By the same token, planets that fall in the first, fourth, seventh, and tenth houses are also considered to be important.

Now here's a rundown on what the houses mean.

Ascendant or Rising: The First of Four Important Critical Angles in a Horoscope

- How other people see you
- How you present yourself to the world
- Your physical appearance

First House: Personality

- Early childhood
- Your ego
- Your body type and how you feel about your body
- General physical health
- Defense mechanisms
- Your creative thrust

Second House: Personal Values

- How you earn and spend your money
- Your personal values
- Your material resources and assets
- Your attitudes and beliefs toward money
- Your possessions and your attitude toward those possessions
- Your self-worth
- Your attitudes about creativity

Third House: Communication and Learning

- Personal expression
- Intellect and mental attitudes and perceptions
- Siblings, neighbors, and relatives
- How you learn
- School until college
- Reading, writing, teaching
- Short trips (the grocery store versus Europe in seven days)
- Earth-bound transportation
- Creativity as a communication device

IC or Fourth House Cusp: The Second Critical Angle in a Horoscope

- Sign on IC describes the qualities and traits of your home during early childhood
- Describes roots of your creative abilities and talents

Fourth House: Your Roots

- Personal/domestic environment
- Your home
- Your attitudes toward family
- Early childhood conditioning
- Real estate
- Your nurturing parent

Some astrologers say this house belongs to Mom or her equivalent in your life, others say it belongs to Dad or his equivalent. It makes sense to us that it's Mom because the fourth house is ruled by the moon, which rules mothers. But in this day and age, when parental roles are in flux, the only hard and fast rule is that the fourth belongs to the parent who nurtures you most of the time.

- The conditions at the end of your life
- Early childhood support of your creativity and interests

Fifth House: Children and Creativity

- Kids, your firstborn in particular
- Love affairs, romance
- What you enjoy
- Creative ability
- Gambling and speculation
- Pets

Traditionally, pets belong in the sixth house. But that definition stems from the days when "pets" were chattel. These days we don't even refer to them as pets. They are animal companions who bring us pleasure.

Sixth House: Work and Responsibility

- Day-to-day working conditions and environment
- Competence and skills
- Your experience of employees and employers
- Duty to work, to employees
- Health and the daily maintenance of your health

Descendant/Seventh House Cusp: The Third Critical Angle in a Horoscope

- The sign on the house cusp describes the qualities sought in intimate or business relationships
- Describes qualities of creative partnerships

Seventh House: Partnerships and Marriage

- Marriage
- Marriage partner
- Significant others
- Business partnerships
- Close friends
- Open enemies
- Contracts

Eighth House: Transformation

- Sexuality as transformation
- Secrets

- Death, taxes, inheritances, insurance, mortgages and loans
- Resources shared with others
- Your partner's finances
- The occult (read: astrology, reincarnation, UFOs, everything weird and strange)
- Your hidden talents
- Psychology
- Life-threatening illnesses
- Your creative depths

Ninth House: Worldview

- Philosophy and religion
- The law, courts, judicial system
- Publishing
- Foreign travels and cultures
- College, graduate school
- Spiritual beliefs
- Travel abroad

MC or Cusp of Tenth House: The Fourth Critical Angle in a Horoscope

- Sign on cusp of MC describes qualities you seek in a profession
- Your public image
- Your creative and professional achievements

Tenth House: Profession and Career

- Public image as opposed to a job that merely pays the bills (sixth house)
- Your status and position in the world
- The authoritarian parent and authority in general
- People who hold power over you
- Your public life
- Your career/profession

Eleventh House: Ideals and Dreams

- Peer groups
- Social circles (your writers' group, your mother's bridge club)
- Your dreams and aspirations
- How you can realize your dreams

Twelfth House: Personal Unconscious

- Power you have disowned that must be claimed again
- Institutions—hospitals, prisons, nursing homes—and what is hidden
- What you must confront this time around, your karma, issues brought in from other lives
- Psychic gifts and abilities
- Healing talents
- What you give unconditionally

In the section on predictions you'll find references to transiting planets moving into certain houses. These houses are actually solar houses that are created by putting your sun sign on the ascendant. This technique is how most predictions are made for the general public rather than for specific individuals.

Lunations

Every year there are twelve new moons and twelve full moons, with some years having thirteen full moons. The extra full moon is called the Blue Moon. New moons are typically when we should begin new projects, set new goals, seek new opportunities. They're times for beginnings. They usher in new opportunities according to house and sign.

Two weeks after each new moon, there's a full moon. This is the time of harvest, fruition, when we reap what we've sown.

Whenever a new moon falls in your sign, take time to brainstorm what you would like to achieve during weeks and months until the full moon falls in your sign. These goals can be in any area of your life. Or you can simply take the time on each new moon to set up goals and strategies for what you would like to achieve or manifest during the next two weeks—until the full moon—or until the next new moon.

Here's a list of all the new moons and full moons during 2014. The asterisk beside any new-moon entry indicates a solar eclipse; the asterisk next to a full-moon entry indicates a lunar eclipse.

TABLE 3
LUNATIONS OF 2014

New Moons

January 1–Capricorn
January 30–Aquarius
March 1–Pisces
March 30–Aries
April 29–Taurus*
May 28–Gemini
June 27–Cancer
July 26–Leo
August 25–Virgo
September 24–Libra
October 23–Scorpio*
November 22–Sagittarius
December 21–Capricorn

Full Moons

January 15–Cancer
February 14–Leo
March 16–Virgo
*April 15–Libra
May 14–Scorpio
June 13–Sagittarius
July 12–Capricorn
August 10–Aquarius
September 8–Pisces
*October 8–Aries
November 6–Taurus
December 6–Gemini

Every year there are two lunar and two solar eclipses, separated from one another by about two weeks. Lunar eclipses tend to deal with emotional issues, our internal world, and often bring an emotional issue to the surface related to the sign and house in which the eclipse falls. They can also result in news. Solar eclipses deal with events and often enable us to see something that has eluded us. They also symbolize beginnings and endings.

Read more about eclipses in the big picture for your sign for 2014. I also recommend Celeste Teal's excellent book, *Eclipses*.

Mercury Retrograde

Every year Mercury—the planet that symbolizes communication and travel—turns retrograde three times. During these periods our travel plans often go awry, communication breaks down, computers go berserk, cars or appliances develop problems. You get the idea. Things in our daily lives don't work as smoothly as we would like.

Here are some guidelines to follow for Mercury retrogrades:

Try not to travel. But if you have to, be flexible and think of it as an adventure. If you're stuck overnight in an airport in Houston or Atlanta, though, the adventure part of this could be a stretch.

Don't sign contracts—unless you don't mind revisiting them when Mercury is direct again.

Communicate as succinctly and clearly as possible.

Back up all computer files. Use an external hard drive and/or a flash drive. If you've had a computer crash, you already know how frustrating it can be to reconstruct your files.

Don't buy expensive electronics. Expensive anything.

Don't submit manuscripts, screenplays, pitch ideas, or launch new projects.

Revise, rewrite, rethink, review.

In the overview for each sign, check out the dates for this year's Mercury retrogrades and how these retrogrades are likely to impact you. Do the same for eclipses.

Other Retrogrades

Every planet except the sun and moon turns retrograde. So let's look at the retrogrades that will occur in 2014.

Venus: Retrograde in Capricorn from January 1 to January 31. This retro is continuation of one that began at the tail end of 2013. Venus retros can cause rough patches in your most intimate relationships. It can also bring about physical inconveniences and discomforts—your AC or heat goes out in the office, at home, or even in your car. Avoid buying luxury items during a Venus retro. That said, good deals can be found during a Venus retrograde. We once bought a car that we traded in a year later for the same price that we paid for it.

Mars: Retrograde in Libra from March 1 to May 19. Since Mars represents your sexuality, ambition, and physicality, best to check your natal chart to find out where you have Libra.

Jupiter: January 1 to March 6, retrograde in Cancer. This retro is a continuation from 2013. During this period your finances may be depressed, your luck factor isn't operating at full potential, and there could be setbacks or delays with publishing and educational ventures. Since the retro falls in Cancer, it's possible there are delays or setbacks at home too.

Saturn: March 2 to July 20. Retrograde in Scorpio. You discover which structures in your life need bolstering. Profits may be depressed.

Uranus: July 21 to December 21. Retrograde in Aries. Upheavals and changes occur, you feel unsettled, you may feel that your uniqueness is being squashed by a situation or relationship.

Neptune: June 9 to November 15. Retrograde in Pisces. Your creativity and ability to envision what you desire are limited in some way.

Pluto: April 14 to September 22. Retrograde in Capricorn. You may feel powerless or unmotivated in some area of your life.

CHAPTER 3

Love and Romance in 2014

Regardless of what kind of craziness is going on in the world around us, we still fall in love, commit to someone, get engaged or married. But our lives are certainly influenced by our environments, and in changing times we may become more independent or needier, our priorities may shift, or we may reach out for new relationships because we have outgrown the old ones. Or they may have outgrown us.

Let's start with your natal Venus. If you don't know what sign and house Venus was in when you were born, check http://www.astro.com/cgi/ade.cgi and enter your birth data. If you don't know the exact time of your birth, put in twelve noon so you can at least see what sign Venus was in when you were born.

The sign and house placement of your natal Venus tells you a great deal about your capacity for loving another and for being loved and your attitudes about love and romance. It also reveals how you approach your creativity, money, beauty, and females. If you're a Taurus or a Libra, Venus rules your sign, and if you have either of those signs rising, Venus rules your chart. It means the placement of Venus in your natal chart is particularly important.

In a man's chart the sign and house placement of Venus can indicate the kind of women to whom he's attracted. It can also reveal something about his relationship with his daughter, if he has one. In a woman's chart Venus indicates relationships with other women and with a daughter, if she has one.

So let's take a look at what your natal Venus means in terms of its sign and house placement:

Venus in the Signs

Venus in Aries

You take risks in romantic relationships. You tend to be passionate and impulsive and may be somewhat self-centered when it comes to romance and love. You're a terrific initiator when it comes to making money, but your money may go out as fast as it comes in. You're also adept at initiating creative projects, but if you lose interest along the way, you drop the project and move on to something new.

Venus in Taurus

Venus rules Taurus, so it's happy here and functions well. You're a sensuous individual, at times even lusty. You form deep emotional attachments in love and romance, and once you meet the right person are fully committed. You can be exceptionally stubborn about having things your way in a relationship. You attract money and prosperity, particularly if you work actively with your beliefs. Your creative expression is heightened by your sensuality. Once you start something, you're rarely a quitter!

Venus in Gemini

You have great charm and wit and can talk to anyone about anything. Your romantic relationships may not last long, and you may be involved with several people at once. You're not consciously fickle, but you simply get bored easily and move on. Two marriages are possible. On the creative front, you have so many interests and talents that it's sometimes difficult for you to choose what you would like to do most. Self-expression comes easily to you.

Venus in Cancer

You're a nurturing, compassionate individual. Home and marriage are important to you, and your family ties are strong. When you commit to a relationship, you commit completely. But until you're committed, there can be a tendency toward secret love affairs. You nurture your own creative abilities and skills with a resoluteness that others admire. You're not a quitter any more than Venus in Taurus is! You benefit through real estate and land and spend money freely on your home and family.

Venus in Leo

Like Venus in Aries, you have great passion and are ardent in your relationships. Your gregarious nature makes you the life of any party and attracts romantic interests easily and with hardly any effort on your part. In any romantic relationship, though, you like your partner to compliment you, notice you, court, and seduce you. You may have creative talent in the performing arts—theater, dance—or become publicly prominent.

Venus in Virgo

You have discriminating tastes in romantic relationships and may keep a mental list of qualities a partner must have. You're analytical about love—until the right person enters your life and sweeps you away. Then that mental list goes straight out the window. You can be self-critical in a relationship and also critical of your partner or about elements in the relationship. The quest of Venus in Virgo is to polish the diamond until it's the best there is. When it comes to artistic expression, you're a perfectionist, the kind of person who insists that all Ts are crossed. You're exceptionally good at any form of communication.

Venus in Libra

Venus rules this sign, so the planet is happy here, just as it is in Taurus. In romance and love you may have an idealized picture of how things are supposed to be and may bend over backward to make that idealized version happen. You seek harmony and peace in all your relationships—the very things that may elude you. Your artistic strengths are considerable and varied. There may be talent with writing, music, art, photography, or singing. You enjoy beauty in all its forms and don't hesitate to spend money on the things you love.

Venus in Scorpio

You have a passionate, sexual nature and are forever seeking the absolute bottom line in a relationship. When someone interests you, that person's pubic persona isn't enough for you. You dig deeper, scratching way beneath the surface, uncovering the individual's secrets and his or her hidden life. This propensity can lead to stormy relationships until you meet someone who erects strong boundaries. Your creativity springs from the deepest levels of your being and is often inspired. You might, for instance, be a pianist who can't read music and plays entirely by ear. Or you might be an artist who never took an art lesson in your life.

Venus in Sagittarius

Just like Venus in Aries and Leo, the other two fire signs, you love passionately. Your generous nature sometimes prompts you to wear your heart on your sleeve. You seek a partner who loves to travel as much as you do and who shares your love of animals and the arts. But when your personal freedom is threatened in some way, when a relationship makes you feel penned in, your passion cools quickly, and you immediately extricate yourself from the relationship. Creatively you seek the larger picture of whatever you're doing and leave the finer details to others.

Venus in Capricorn

Your capacity for love runs deep, but you are often restrained in how you express it. This restraint may be the result of a lack of trust in yourself or the other person, but it can also simply be one of your patterns, something that began when you were very young. Sexually however all the restraints and reserve fall away and your true passions burst forth. You strive to achieve financial and material assets and work hard to do so.

Venus in Aquarius

For you love and romance must start with an intellectual camaraderie, an exchange of ideas. You enjoy the company of idiosyncratic individuals, people out of the mainstream who have unusual ideas, occupations, or perceptions. You have many friends and among them may be a person who interests you romantically. In romantic relationships you need intellectual stimulation. Your financial habits could be erratic, or you may earn your living in an unusual way. Creatively you're a trendsetter.

Venus in Pisces

Your compassionate nature is practically legendary among people who know you. In love you're a true romantic, the kind of person who enjoys moonlit walks on beaches. It's this idealism, though, that sometimes gets you into trouble if the reality doesn't measure up. In a relationship your sensitivity to your partner's moods often borders on psychic. Romantic relationships and emotional attachments are necessary for your well-being.

Venus in the Houses

First house

You're a natural charmer, friendly, and probably physically attractive. You may have some unique talent that finds expression in art or music. You love literature and poetry and have a fondness for beautiful surroundings. This placement is usually fortunate — unless Venus is poorly aspected — and things generally come to you with ease. The closer Venus is to the ascendant — the rising — the more pronounced these qualities are.

Second house

Financial comfort, perhaps even wealth. You benefit financially from marriage and partnerships. You're probably an extravagant spender, but you can usually afford it, so it's not an issue. Your personal values are important to you, and you spend time and effort developing them.

Third house

You converse easily with people and are comfortable in your neighborhood or community. You're close to your siblings, other relatives, and neighbors and have excellent rapport with your immediate family. The love of your life may be someone you meet in your community or through relatives.

Fourth house

Your home and family are important to you and vital to your well-being. You seek harmony in your domestic environment and go to great lengths to maintain it. It's possible that you meet the love of your life early in life and then meet again later on when you're adults. You have a great rapport with your parents and gain financially through them. The closer Venus is to the cusp of the fourth house, the more pronounced these attributes will be.

Fifth house

For love, romance, children, and creative endeavors, this is where Venus is really at home. The fifth-house placement is great for happy love affairs, artistic projects, and anything creative. Your children may have unusual talents. You gain through romantic partners, children, and any sort of creative endeavor. Your undoing may be excessive pleasure!

Sixth house

Your daily work is a source of pleasure for you. You enjoy what you do, whatever it is, and probably have harmonious relationships with your coworkers. You're able to integrate your creativity into your daily work, and other people appreciate and admire your work.

This placement favors good health generally, but you should avoid excessive use of alcohol and drugs. In terms of romance you may work with the one you love!

Seventh house

Venus is happy here. It's likely that you'll have a happy marriage and profitable partnerships generally. You and your partner may work together in some capacity, perhaps moving toward a common goal— self-employment, for instance. You're a magnet for attracting what you need in partnerships and financial benefits.

Eighth house

You gain financially through marriage and partnerships, inheritances, taxes, and contracts. You're lucky when it comes to other people's money and resources. You may have unusual and positive experiences with metaphysics. Love and romance with someone you knew in a past life are possible.

Ninth house

Romance and love may find you while you're traveling overseas. Music and art with spiritual themes intrigue you, and you may have talent yourself in these areas. This placement of Venus favors involvement with publishing, spiritual groups, higher education, and foreign travel.

Tenth house

Talk about popularity! Writers, artists, entertainers, actors, novelists, reporters, and diplomats are all indicated by this placement. You're at ease in any kind of social venue, and other people are attracted to you and your ideas. Career matters and your professional life generally tend to unfold smoothly with little effort on your part. You may be "married" to your career or find love with someone who works in your profession. The closer Venus falls to the cusp of the tenth house, the more pronounced the qualities.

Eleventh house

Friendships and groups are important to you. They help you to achieve your wishes and dreams and share your interests in the arts, music, and books. You invest a lot of time and energy in your friendships, particularly with women, and could meet someone special through friends.

Twelfth house

Secret love affairs and romantic intrigues are indicated. You may work in solitude or behind the scenes in some sort of artistic profession. You enjoy mystery and adventure and actually enjoy the dramas of romantic intrigues.

Venus Transits and Retrogrades

Unless Venus is retrograde, as it is in 2014, a Venus transit lasts from three to four weeks. The times to watch for are when Venus returns to the place where it was when you were born and when Venus conjuncts your sun.

The first period is called a Venus return and is usually a genuinely enjoyable period. You have all the support you need or want from friends and partners. Everything that is promised in the natal placement of Venus is enhanced.

The second period is also terrific. It enhances all the qualities of your sun sign, bolsters your self-confidence, artistic inspirations, and ambitions and should do wonders for your love life.

In 2014 Venus begins the year retrograde in Capricorn and turns direct on January 31. These retrograde periods can be tough on your love life and your artistic expression. Or you may find yourself dealing with issues from the past in either of these areas. Another possibility with Venus retrograde is that your physical comfort may be compromised in some way. Perhaps the air conditioning or heat in your office building goes on the fritz, or maybe the defroster, heat, or AC in your car stops working.

This year, Venus transits Capricorn twice—at the beginning of the year and again briefly at the end. In between it moves through all the other signs as well. For specifics on how Venus transits affect your sign, read chapter 14.

CHAPTER 4

Finances in 2014

More than four years after the financial meltdown in 2008—when the "too big to fail" banks were bailed out, the housing market bottomed out, and unemployment burgeoned—the situation hasn't improved.

According to www.forecasts.org, unemployment by the spring of 2012 is supposed to be at 10.3 percent, and unless the economy turns around, that figure may be much higher by 2014. Despite the Obama administration's "homeowner bailout" programs, six million Americans are either behind on their mortgage payments or facing foreclosure, and millions more are underwater on their mortgages. An article in the *Las Vegas Sun* estimates that as of late 2011 American homeowners owe $700 billion to $800 billion more than their homes are actually worth.

A report in Huffington Post in October 2011 revealed half of borrowers with prime loans—those loans made to individuals with good credit and income—will likely end up underwater. A Fitch ratings report found that with home prices expected to drop in value by another 10 percent, at least half of prime borrowers will end up underwater. Complicating the situation, of course, are unemployment, underemployment, and the rising costs of goods.

How fast are those costs rising? Do your own test. What products do you use regularly? How much have their prices risen in the past year? A year ago our favorite coffee, a Cuban brand, used to sell for $2.59 a pound. The price has doubled. A dozen eggs that cost a buck a year ago are now twice that. A loaf of bread that used to cost a buck now costs three times that. You get the idea here, and you've no doubt noticed the rise in costs in your own life just for basics. When you include the prices of gasoline, electricity, tuition for college, and everything else, it's no wonder the middle class is shrinking.

The reality points to a pattern that has been prevalent throughout the twenty-first century—greed. Whether it's corporate or individual greed, there are no free rides. Banks lent to people who didn't have the income to meet mortgage payments and bundled good and bad mortgages together and sold them off. Borrowers used their homes as ATM machines. In a sense what is happening to the American economy is a reflection of what has happened to the U.S. economy overall: we are living beyond our means.

On the other hand, there are plenty of homeowners who weren't living beyond their means but whose lives changed dramatically when they were laid off or got sick, or their income was somehow diminished. You probably know people in your own community who have suffered in this way.

So what do all these depressing statistics means for you in 2014? A couple of things. If you've been hit badly by this economy, the first thing you should so is become politically active. It's not enough to vote in elections. Democracy is also about expressing your opinion. Occupy Wall Street started as a genuine grassroots movement and hit a nerve with the nation's young people. What started as a small protest on September 17, 2011, became a global movement within a month. That kind of activism is what helps to usher in a change in the status quo.

Take stock of your particular abilities and talents. Is there something you can do that would fill a niche in the market? Adversity, after all, can be an opportunity that prompts you to perceive your own skills in a different way and to see the market with new eyes.

What can you change about the way you live? Do you stash away a percentage of everything you make? Do you spend money as quickly as it comes in? Do you have a realistic budget? Are you in credit card debt? Do you live debt free? Depending on your financial situation, here are tips for each sign on how to maximize your potential this year; when the stars favor your finances—and when they don't.

But first take this inventory about your beliefs concerning money.

Belief Inventory

Here's a list of some commonly held negative beliefs about money. Check the ones to which you subscribe:

- Money is the root of all evil
- Money is nonspiritual

- The rich have major problems in their lives
- Money corrupts
- If you have too much money, you have to worry about losing it
- If you have too much money, it takes over your life.
- The wealthy don't have money problems, but they have a lot of other problems.

Many of these beliefs we've adopted from family and peers and have held on to them because they're comfortable, we believe they're true, or because we don't even realize we believe them! So if you're not satisfied with what you're earning, start monitoring how you think about money. Any time you find yourself thinking a negative thought about money, turn the thought around by thinking something more positive. Also, read Napoleon Hills' classic *Think and Grow Rich* and *Money and the Law of Attraction* by Esther and Jerry Hicks.

Now let's take a look at how you can maximize your earning potential in 2014.

Aries

There's a reason you're called the trailblazer, the entrepreneur. You see opportunities where others may not and figure out a way to turn those opportunities into money. You're the type who, in the midst of the Great Depression, might have launched your own business and filled a gap you recognized in the market. Adversity doesn't scare you; it becomes your booster rocket.

There are two excellent periods this year for finances. The first period falls between May 2 and 28, when Venus is in your sign. This period is excellent for earning additional money, sales, and asking for a raise. The second period, when Venus transits Taurus and your financial area, falls between May 28 and June 23. During this period you may be more prone toward saving rather than spending. But if you do feel the urge to spend, it may be for high-end items—art, jewelry. So if you succumb to the urge, be sure to pay cash!

Although we talk about Jupiter transits in a later chapter, this planet's transit through fellow fire sign Leo could be quite nice for your finances. That time frame: July 16, 2014, to August 11, 2015.

Excellent backup dates: September 13 to October 26, when Mars transits fellow fire sign Sagittarius.

Taurus

Many of you are artistic, good with money and investments, fashion, the culinary arts, photography, writing, music. In fact, you probably have numerous talents but because you tend to be somewhat reserved, other people don't know about them. Well, now is the time to let your true self shine, Taurus. And once you do, once you embrace all you are, then the opportunities begin to arrive, and you may have a chance to earn your living doing what you love.

An excellent time this year for maximizing your earning potential falls between May 28 and June 23, when Venus is in your sign. This period is one in which you feel extremely good about yourself and life in general, and that feeling bolsters your self-confidence. Others pick up on this, and suddenly, Taurus, you can do no wrong. You get hired for that job you want; you land a promotion or raise; you sell your novel.

The next period that could pay off financially falls between January 1 and July 16, when Jupiter transits Cancer, a water sign compatible with your earth-sign sun. This occurs in your solar third house of communication and travel. No telling what treasures you may discover during this transit. Perhaps your Web site wins an award. Or you sell your novel. Or you become a travel writer.

Good backup dates: October 26 to December 4, when Mars transits fellow earth sign Capricorn, your solar ninth house. Your ambitions lead you in new directions—perhaps overseas, into publishing, or higher education. Maybe law school is in your future!

Gemini

Left to your own devices, things like checkbooks and saving accounts and IRAs and investments are for other people to ponder, such as your accountant, partner, parents, or sibling. You would rather write and talk about *ideas.* So let's talk about the *idea* of money. What does it actually represent to you? Energy? Freedom? Albatross? During 2014 it's to your advantage to look at money as energy and freedom. The more you make, the greater your freedom to do what interests you. The more effort you expend, the greater the energy you're putting into what you do and the greater the return. At least that's how it's supposed to work in theory. But you have to remain focused and resolute.

Most Geminis are versatile and adaptable, and many are excellent communicators. How can you use those particular skills and talents to earn an income?

One of your best times this year for increasing your earnings falls between January 1 and July 16, when Jupiter transits Cancer, your solar second house of finances. This transit has been going on since 2013, so by now you should have a clear idea how it works and the kind of luck and expansion that accompanies it.

Another excellent period for increasing your earnings occurs between June 23 and July 18, when Venus transits your sign. Things may seem to be going so well that you could be tempted to kick back and chill. Resist that temptation! Use this time frame to move forward—ask for a raise, apply for a promotion, or look for a new job that pays more.

An excellent backup period is September 13 to October 26, when Mars transits fire sign Sagittarius, your solar seventh house. This transit could bring exactly the right business partner you need. Or you and your spouse or partner go into business together.

Cancer

Your imagination and intuition should serve you well this year, particularly if you use both to expand your income. You tend to be good at budgeting your money and usually know what you earn, spend, and on what. Even though you probably aren't obsessed about money, you find a sense of security in having money in savings that you can draw on when you need to.

This year there are several periods that favor your finances. The first occurs between July 18 and August

12, when Venus transits your sign. During this period ask for a raise or promotion, apply for new jobs, network with professional peers, or open an IRA. Lucky you, this transit occurs just after the Mercury retrograde in your sign ends. Those dates: June 7 to July 1. Reread the section on Mercury retrogrades in chapter 2.

The second period when your finances—and just about everything else in your life—may undergo radical expansion occurs between January 1 and July 16, while expansive Jupiter transits your sign. This transit has been going on since last June, so you undoubtedly have a good idea already about the kinds of events and opportunities that Jupiter often brings.

Excellent backup dates: August 12 to September 5, when Venus transits Leo and your financial area. This period could bring a new source of income.

Leo

In 2014 the secret to staying afloat financially is twofold. First, have the facts at your fingertips. Know how much you actually bring home after taxes and FICA and any other fees that are automatically deducted from your income. Can you live on your take-home pay? If not, where can you cut back in your budget? Do you and your partner eat out frequently? Is it necessary? Do you go on shopping sprees? Keep track of your expenses for a couple of weeks for a more accurate picture of what comes in—and goes out.

Second, as one of the most flamboyant and theatrical signs of the zodiac, you probably like to look your best when in public. Be sure to budget for that—

clothing, shoes, hairstylists, spas—whatever it takes to maintain your public persona. But instead of shopping at the upscale shops, perhaps you can do equally well in thrift stores.

There are some excellent periods in 2014 for increasing your earnings. The first period falls between August 12 and September 5, when Venus transits your sign. This one boosts self-confidence, other people find you infinitely appealing, and you can do no wrong, Leo. So ask for a raise or promotion or send out résumés. Unexpected bonuses or royalties could arrive during this time. If so, stash the money in an IRA.

The next period falls between July 16, 2014, and August 11, 2015, when Jupiter transits your sign. Expansive Jupiter seeks to improve your life in all areas during this transit.

Excellent backup dates: September 5 to 29, when Venus moves through Virgo, your financial area. This period favors details and enables you to connect all the dots.

Virgo

You're the most discriminating of signs—measured, diligent, with a penchant for details. You can be something of a perfectionist too, but rarely demand of others what you demand of yourself. Whatever you take on, you do so with complete dedication. So in 2014 perfect your finances, Virgo. Set your monetary goals and then figure out how best to achieve them.

One of the most favorable periods for earning more falls between September 5 and 29, when Venus transits your sign. This period is favorable for landing a raise or promotion, for receiving money from unexpected sources—an insurance payment, a royalty check—and for sending out résumés for a job that pays you more. It's also good for pitching manuscripts and screenplays.

Another potentially profitable period occurs between January 1 and July 16, when expansive Jupiter transits compatible water sign Cancer and forms a beneficial angle to your sun. Friends and any groups to which you belong prove helpful. This period is when you're in the right place at the right time to bolster your bank account, land a raise, or make money by expanding your services or products to overseas markets.

Excellent backup dates: September 29 to October 23, when Venus transits Libra, your financial area.

Libra

Your sign, like Taurus, is Venus ruled, so its transits are particularly important to you. You feel more comfortable and balanced when surrounded by beauty—fresh flowers, art, pleasing furniture, perhaps even some sort of unique collection that has good memories attached to it. Music and books may be important to you too, and perhaps some of your disposable income goes toward these things.

Between September 29 and October 23 Venus transits your sign. This period should be particularly good for you. Venus is happy in your sign and can help you to bring in additional income from a variety of different sources. If you're in sales, you can sell anything to anyone. You might sell a manuscript, piece of art, or some other product born of your creativity.

During Jupiter's transit of compatible fire sign Leo, between July 16, 2014, and August 11, 2015, you may experience an expansion in your income that seems to happen without any effort on your part. That's an illusion, of course. You have been seeding the possibilities for quite a while now. Jupiter means expansion, and its energy can be used wherever you apply your attention and energy.

Excellent backup dates: March 1 to May 19, when Mars is in direct motion in your sign. This one acts like a booster rocket!

Scorpio

As a fixed water sign and the most emotionally intense sign in the zodiac, you're no stranger to transformation. With Pluto as the ruler of your sign, your life is constantly undergoing transformation of some kind. But if you would like to bolster and transform your finances, 2014 is a great year to do it. Your considerable intuition and ability to get to the absolute bottom line of anything you research and investigate serve you well this year.

Between October 23 and November 16 Venus transits your sign. So during this period ask for a raise, apply for a promotion, or send out résumés for jobs that really interest you. Be proactive. You and your ideas appeal to others. Your charisma intrigues them, so use it to your advantage.

Another excellent period for expanding your income occurs between January 1 and July 16, 2014, when Jupiter transits fellow water sign Cancer and forms a beneficial angle to your sun. This period should be productive for you, with new creative opportunities that could bring in additional income.

Saturn begins the year in your sign, Scorpio, which should bring stability and structure to your finances and other areas of your life. It's retrograde between March 2 and July 20, so it essentially enters a dormant state during this period. But before the retrograde and afterward, until it enters Sagittarius on December 23, use its energy to build a more solid financial foundation for yourself.

Excellent backup dates: July 25 to September 13, when Mars, your coruler, transits your sign. This one is your booster rocket and confers enormous physical energy and resolve.

Sagittarius

Let the good times roll . . . and roll! As a mutable fire sign, your life is about activity and forward motion. You don't have time for things like budgets, balancing a checkbook, and keeping track of what you earn and spend. Then when it's time to do your taxes, you freak out. You can't find receipts, your files are messed up . . . you get the idea.

In 2013 we advised you to organize your finances. If you did that, in 2014 your finances should be much easier to navigate. You'll be alert for the periods when it will be easier to increase your income. More money means more travel, and any Sadge loves that idea!

Between November 16 and December 10 Venus transits your sign. Not only does your self-confidence soar, but others find you appealing and want you on their team. So ask for a raise or promotion, pitch your ideas, or submit your manuscript or screenplay or some other product you have created.

Between January 31 and March 5 and December 10, 2014, and January 4, 2015, Venus in direct motion transits Capricorn, your financial area. These two periods should prompt you to be careful with your money, particularly as your income increases. Just because you have more money in your pocket, Sadge, doesn't mean it should go out as quickly as it comes in. Capricorn is a grounded, focused sign, and as Venus moves through it you learn the wisdom of saving.

Another excellent period for you and your money should occur during Jupiter's thirteen-month transit through fellow fire sign Leo. This one should increase not only your finances but also opportunities in whatever area you place your attention.

Capricorn

As a cardinal earth sign, you build your financial world just as you do everything else, one brick at a time. You do it patiently, methodically, and usually have a goal in mind—double your earnings in six months, for instance. Or pay off your mortgage in the next two years.

In 2014 you have several windows of opportunity when it's easier to increase your earnings, launch a business, pitch an idea that someone will buy, or sell a book. Luck is on your side; you're in the right place at the right time; you meet exactly the right people who make things happen. The first period falls between January 31 and March 5; the second period is between December 10, 2014, and January 4, 2015, when Venus is moving direct through your sign. This transit is a confidence booster. When you feel good about yourself, others pick up on it, and suddenly everything flows your way. If you're looking for a better-paying job or a second job, then this period could bring news.

The second period occurs between January 1 and July 16 when Jupiter transits your opposite sign, Cancer. This transit should expand your professional partnerships, which in turn could be very positive for your finances.

You have an additional plus this year. Saturn is in Scorpio until December 23, forming a strong and beneficial angle to your sun. This transit helps you to build solid financial foundations.

Aquarius

You don't really fit into any financial category. Some Aquarians are great with money; others aren't. Some are savers; others are spenders. But one thing is for sure. When you make up your mind to do something, you do it. No one and nothing can sway you from a path you've chosen. So for 2014 let's look at times when your income can increase.

One of the most favorable periods falls between March 5 and April 5. Venus transits your sign, suggesting that your appeal is broad and others like you and your ideas, making this an ideal time to ask for a raise. Ask with the expectation that the raise will be given. Whether you're sending out résumés or interviewing for jobs, you're in your element and should reap the rewards you so justly deserve.

Another good period falls between April 5 and

May 2, when Venus moves through Pisces, your financial area. You may have a tough time making up your mind if you're given choices about your money. But once you do make up your mind, this transit could bring about a raise, result in the repayment of a loan, or perhaps bring in an insurance payment or tax break.

Excellent backup dates: December 4, 2014, to January 12, 2015. Mars is in your sign, and it's your booster rocket, Aquarius.

Pisces

Your considerable imagination and intuition will prove enormously valuable in this year of transformation. Whatever you can imagine, after all, can manifest itself. So if you're imagining a quantum leap in your income, Pisces, fix a figure firmly in mind, focus on it, release it — and let the universe figure out the connections that must be made for you to earn that amount of money.

In the interim, of course, it's smart not to just sit back but to become more proactive. If you dislike your job, figure out what you would like to be doing and start submitting applications and résumés. If you often find yourself short of money, set up a realistic budget and try to stick to it. You know, do the small stuff!

Timing is essential, so let's take a look at the windows of opportunity in 2014 when things really flow your way. These periods are when you should ask for a raise or promotion, submit résumés, schedule interviews, do whatever you can to earn more. The first period falls between April 5 and May 2, when Venus transits your sign. This is when you're more you than ever! Turn on the charm, let your muse in 24/7.

The second period falls between January 1 and July 16, when expansive Jupiter transits fellow water sign Cancer and forms a beneficial angle to your sun. Expansion, luck, you're in the right place at the right time!

CHAPTER 5

Lunar Madness in 2014

Collective Concepts of the Moon

There is something truly magical about the moon. As the closest celestial body to Earth, it has captured man's imagination for millennia. It has been the stuff of myths and fairy tales, poetry and legends. It has been worshipped and cursed and endowed with magical and curative powers. Religions have grown up around it. Sacrifices have been made to it.

In ancient cultures the passage of time was marked according to the lunation—or cycle—of the moon. A *month* was the time between one new moon and the next, and in a typical year there were thirteen lunar cycles. This way of marking time still exists among some pagan sects and may be closer to our natural rhythms than our present solar calendar.

Early shamans may have timed certain rituals according to the phases of the moon. Tribal people often planted crops during a new moon and harvested at a full moon. In the eighth century B.C. various civilizations discarded their 360-day calendar and based the calendar on observations of the sky. In ancient Rome priests observed the heavens and were supposed to announce to the emperor when a new month began. The month usually began with a new moon. This practice was also used by the Celts and Babylonians.

In the early fifties the moon was a favorite theme in science fiction books and movies, and the storylines rarely varied: the aliens came from the moon, we colonized the moon, or the moon fell out of orbit . . . you get the general picture. Even Disney issued movies in which the moon played a vital role. In one film, a Western, a woman who wore a hoop skirt typical of the American west started bouncing and kept bouncing higher and higher until she bounced right into the moon. The shadow you see in the moon is, according to Disney, that woman in the hoop skirt.

In 1969 Neil Armstrong took one giant leap for mankind, and our concept of the moon was forever changed. Even though its relative position in the sky hadn't changed, everything else about it had.

We now had some idea what it really looked like, and the news was far from good. Dust, dust, and more dust. A black vacuum. Unimaginable cold. Nothingness. What's most vivid in our minds, though, is how the Earth looked from the moon—a swirling turquoise gem 240,000 miles distant, a blue pearl turning in space. Our planet literally looked alive.

This was the year when Vietnam was in full swing. Americans arrived home in body bags, riots swept across college campuses, LSD was the drug of choice. People were tuning in and dropping out faster than the pictures of the moon were beamed back to earth.

This was the year that half a million people converged on the tiny town of Woodstock, New York, to hear Hendrix, Baez, Dylan, Joplin, and all the other musicians who had captured the emotional reality of war and chaos. Women threw off their shackles. Carlos Castaneda and Aldous Huxley hurled open the doors to other realities. Camelot was dead, Martin Luther King was dead, and we had walked on the moon.

In many ways those steps of Armstrong's signaled that we were ready to confront our unconscious selves, our feminine, intuitive selves.

Fast-forward to the summer of 1997, July 4 to be exact. In the opening scenes of the movie *Independence Day* a mammoth shadow falls across the surface of the moon. A moving shadow whose shape is unmistakable. The message comes through loud and clear: the shadow is that of a spaceship that uses the moon as a base, and now that ship is on the move toward Earth. What ensues is pure Hollywood, with Will Smith holding the record for aliens annihilated. But *Independence Day*, like Armstrong's one giant leap, is part of our contemporary, collective perceptions of the moon, its essential beauty and sublime mysteries.

Despite Hollywood and NASA, each of us has some personal concept about the moon. After all, we drop our heads back on any given night, and there it is, shaped like a ubiquitous eye or the grin of a Cheshire cat or like a piece of fruit with the top lopped off. It speaks to us. We speak to it. Romance, madness, werewolves, witches, pagans, Druids, ocean tides and blood tides, or a sharp rise in murder and mayhem: it's all fair game where the moon is concerned. Every notion that we hold about the moon is true *for us,* and that subjective texture is certainly in keeping with the nature of the moon in astrology.

If the sun is where you shine in your corner of the universe, the moon is your personal oracle. If the sun represents your life force, the moon represents the internal landscape that supports and maintains the life force. In astrology lunar energy is embodied in that mythological moment when Luke Skywalker recognizes that Darth Vader is his father or when, in *ET,* the alien is getting drunk and the boy is trying to dissect a frog at school and their psyches mesh. Lunar energy is operating when reality splits off for the character Gwyneth Paltrow plays in *Sliding Doors* or during the love scene in *Titanic.*

Lunar energy is the MO in *Thelma and Louise, Jacob's Ladder,* and *What Dreams May Come.* It's the psychic visions the young boy has in *The Shining* or the visions another young boy has in *The Sixth Sense.* It's the mother's anguish in *The Deep End of the Ocean.* Without lunar energy we would be empty shells, automatons, the burn-the-books society in *Fahrenheit 451.* We would be Keanu Reeves still stuck in the matrix, powerless puppets who accept everything at face value.

Lunar Facts and Oddities

Most of us learn facts about the moon in grade-school science class. Today's kids have a distinct advantage over their parents of course because we've already been to the moon, and information is so readily accessible through the Internet.

The moon is our only satellite, and its average distance from Earth is 238,857 miles. Its revolution around the Earth takes twenty-seven days, seven hours, and forty-three minutes. Even though it's only a quarter the size of Earth, its gravitational pull is the main cause of our ocean tides. In fact, the moon actually has more than twice the effect on tides than the sun.

Since our bodies are primarily water, the moon's gravitational pull on the tides also affects our bodily fluids, metabolic rates, and of course our emotions. The link, for instance, between the full moon and violent aggression has been noted for years by police officers, hospital workers, and employees at mental institutions.

In the 1970s a Miami psychiatrist, Arnold Lieber, decided to conduct a scientific study to find out if these observations were true. As a med student at Jackson Memorial Hospital in Miami he'd noticed recurring periods when patients on the psyche ward were more disturbed than usual. These periods would last for several days, then the patients would resume their normal behavior. He became curious about the phenomenon and finally conducted a scientific study. His findings, later backed by four other independent studies, confirmed that during the full moon and, to a lesser extent, the new moon, there are increases in all violent crimes—homicide, rape, assault. There's also an increase in lesser crimes—burglary, auto theft, larceny, and drunken and disorderly behavior.

Is it any coincidence, then, that the word *lunatic* is derived from the word *lunar*?

Hospital workers and maternity ward nurses have

long noticed that more babies are born at the full and new moons than at any other time of the month. These may be due to the fact that the gravitational pull is strongest when the moon, sun, and Earth are aligned, as they are during the new and full moons. These observations have been backed by scientific studies. Interestingly enough, the lunar calendar is still the basis for calculating a pregnancy. The nine months are synodic months (the length of time it takes the moon to orbit Earth).

Since the moon has no atmosphere, it has nothing to protect it from meteor strikes, which is why its surface is pocked with impact craters. Since it has no tectonic or volcanic activity, its surface is immune to the erosive effects of atmospheric weathering, tectonic shifts, and volcanic upheavals that reshape the surface of our planet. In comparison, Earth is a work in progress. On the moon, even the footprints left by the Apollo astronauts will remain intact for millions of years unless a meteor strike obliterates them.

The moon's gravity is about a sixth of ours; that's why the Apollo astronauts looked like they were jumping rope up there. Despite appearances to the contrary, the moon has no light of its own. That gorgeous full moon you see each month is the reflected light of our sun.

Astrological Lunar Facts

The moon in your horoscope is every bit as important as your sun sign. In fact, Eastern astrologers give the moon greater emphasis than the sun sign. The moon rules the sign of Cancer and the fourth house in the horoscope. It represents mom or whoever plays that role for you and also symbolizes other women in your life. The moon is feminine, yin, our intuitive selves.

In the physical body her territory pertains primarily to women—breasts, ovaries, womb. In both genders she rules internal fluids and the stomach, and of course she's our emotional barometer, the gauge of our inner health. Not surprisingly, the moon rules conception.

A Czech physician, in fact, theorized that every woman had a fertility cycle that depended on the phase of the moon when she was born. Eugene Jones developed a fertilization calendar based on his theory, which allegedly showed a 98 percent success rate. He charged an astronomical fee for his calendar, but people who were desperate for children paid it.

Jones claimed that if a woman used his methods, she could choose the gender of her child. His technique was based on the rules of classical astrology, which he'd studied, and boils down to using the gender of moon signs. If conception took place on a Leo day, the child would be male. On a Taurus day, the child would be a girl.

The medical establishment went berserk over his claims. But when a panel of gynecologists challenged him to predict the genders of babies based only on their conception dates, Jones' accuracy was 87 percent.

If you don't know the sign of your natal moon, check on any of the astrology sites listed in this book and get a free birth chart. You'll need your exact time of birth, place, and of course the date!

The Transiting Moon

The moon changes signs every two and a half days. As you follow along in the daily prediction section for your sign, you'll be able to keep tabs on where the moon is on any given day. In the daily predictions we note when the moon is new or full. New moons favor new beginnings. Quite often around the time of the new moon you may receive good news about a project, relationship, or a financial or family matter. Full moons often coincide with completions, culminations, and news that ties up loose ends.

Certain activities are favored on certain lunar days, so let's take a look at how you can maximize the transiting moon's energy in your life.

Aries Moon

Cardinal Fire Sign

This is the day to be a fearless entrepreneur, to move forward on projects that have been sitting on the back burner for weeks or months. It's a great time to initiate new projects too, especially those that have been rattling around in the back of your head for some time.

You may feel restless and impatient with others, so the best way to deal with it is to pour that energy into something about which you feel passionate. Others see you as a leader, as the person with answers. You attract individuals who are eager to be on your team. You feel more self-sufficient, capable of doing whatever needs to be done.

Follow your impulses regardless of how odd they may seem. Sometimes our impulses are the universe's way of leading us toward a new opportunity, relationship, or creative project. Since Mars rules Aries, physical activity is heightened. Take a yoga class. Join the gym. Go walking. Weather permitting, it's a great day for a hike, bike ride, or long swim.

It's a good day to *believe* that whatever you desire can manifest itself. Your intentions and focus are key.

Taurus Moon

Fixed Earth Sign

The moon loves Taurus as much as it loves Cancer, the sign that it rules. In Taurus lunar energies work effortlessly and smoothly, and that makes your intuition easier to develop and use.

On a Taurus moon day think about that children's story *Ferdinand the Bull*. The author probably wasn't thinking about Taurus when he created the character, but Ferdinand is the perfect archetype for Taurus. Ferdinand enjoyed peaceful surroundings, and today so do you. In fact, peacefulness and harmony are vital to your emotional well-being. You need these qualities the way a Gemini moon needs books or education or communication with other people.

It will take a lot to anger you today, but repeated provocation can trigger your "bull's rush" fury, the human equivalent of Ferdinand's reaction to the bee sting. Some of the things that can set you off are incessant nagging by someone who wants you to do something you don't want to do, insistence that you act in a particular way, unreasonable demands or actions by anyone.

A Taurus moon day enables you to stick with something right to the end. You won't be a quitter. You will also be slow to change your mind and opinion and won't be rushed or cajoled into doing something that doesn't interest you.

If you enjoy gardening or have a particular artistic passion, then today is the day to indulge!

Gemini Moon

Mutable Air Sign

Today your nemesis is boredom. Its possibility unnerves you. If you were put in a bare room without windows, books, TV, radio, computer, paper or pen, phone, fax, or anything else, you would freak within the hour. This may be true of the other air-sign moons as well, but for the Gemini moon it's a sure thing. Your emotional well-being needs mental stimulation and the means to communicate with others.

It's a good day to start blogging, if you haven't already, to dust off that old manuscript you were working on way back when, or to get together with friends and shoot the breeze. You may feel compelled to sign up for a workshop or even an online course in something that interests you. Or you may decide to go to college or graduate school. It's a great day for research, for delving into a topic or concern and finding out everything you can about it.

Communication, whatever form is takes, is paramount.

Cancer Moon

Cardinal Water Sign

Today your memories work overtime. You're able to conjure sights, smells, tastes, sounds, and textures from your past in vivid detail. The event you're recalling may have happened thirty years ago, but in your memory it's just as fresh and detailed as the day it happened.

The moon rules Cancer, so it's at home in this sign. This is where its energies express themselves most smoothly. Today your emotions are racing through you, and it may be easy to have your feelings hurt. Your acute sensitivity makes you feel vulnerable, and it isn't easy for you to step back and view a situation or relationship dispassionately.

Family, home, and roots are especially important to you today. Schedule time to be with the people you love. Whether it's a traditional family or friends whom you love like family, you draw comfort and sustenance from these individuals. It's a good time to work on creative projects; your inspiration comes from deep places within you. During the Cancer moon you may have a real soft spot for animals—strays that drop by your place for a bowl of food, the neighbor's cat that sneaks into your house. A visit to your local pound may be in order!

Leo Moon

Fixed Fire Sign

It's a perfect day to showcase your talents. In fact when you enter a room, people notice you. If for some reason they don't, you make sure that they do. This isn't just an ego thing, either. Applause and being noticed are vital to your well-being today even if your only audience is your family. *You need to be recognized as someone special.*

Your flair for drama today is remarkable. It runs throughout everything you do—from the way you dress, speak, and act to the activities in which you engage. You may decide to take in a play or try out for a part. Creatively you're at the top of your game, and anything you undertake will bear this dramatic stamp.

It's a good time to spend time with your kids doing something everyone enjoys, volunteer at an animal shelter, get out and be seen, socialize, make new contacts. Network. Be as flamboyant as you can imagine.

Virgo Moon

Mutable Earth Sign

Today you're in a quest for perfection, and the words *Be the best that you can* take on a whole new dimension of meaning. You thrive on order and manage to use today's lunar energy to tackle emotional chaos in your life and impose order on it.

Virgo tends to be a health-oriented sign, so today favors starting a new diet, nutritional program, or exercise regimen. Even if you're already involved in these areas, consider fine-tuning the details. You also may want to consider blogging or writing about what you're learning about health, nutrition, and exercise.

Today also favors performing a service for someone else—not for pay, not with any thought of compensation, but as a good deed. This could mean anything from volunteering at your favorite charity to putting in some time at an animal rescue sanctuary. Pay attention to your spiritual beliefs today. Are you in tune with a greater good? Are your thoughts the most positive they can be?

Libra Moon

Cardinal Air Sign

Among astrologers certain moon signs stir the soul for the sheer beauty of what they represent. The Taurus moon is one of these. The Libra moon is another.

Today at the heart of it you're a lover, a true romantic. Moonlit beaches, bouquets of roses, books of poetry, going to the opera, a summer rain: this is the language your soul speaks during the Libra moon. So first of all surround yourself with beauty today—music, scenery, people. Just the sight of all this beauty will deepen your appreciation for life.

It's a good day for group work—in your community or with your students, peers, or fellow workers. Or it's a great time to socialize and network. Today your interests tend toward people and relationships, your artistic interests, and attaining peace and harmony. You can see both sides of an issue with greater clarity, and try to avoid conflict.

The Libra moon can enhance your intuition, so try to follow your hunches today and see where they lead you. If you don't meditate yet, today is a terrific time to start. It doesn't have to be lengthy. In fact, five minutes in a quiet place, with your mind still, is all you need. You'll come out of it refreshed. Keep track of any impressions that come your way during those five minutes.

If you're in a committed relationship, be sure to take time today to spend time with your partner. Have a romantic dinner at home or at your favorite restaurant. Talk, converse, get in touch with each other.

Scorpio Moon

Fixed Water Sign

Emotionally it's a powerful day. You feel everything so intensely that it's as if some new, inner part of you has awakened from a deep sleep. You may feel as if you've been seized by a force beyond your control. Despite how it feels, this sense of outside forces is just an illusion. Your emotions are your most powerful allies today. They provide you with a direct, immediate connection to the deepest parts of your intuitive self and are capable of instantly transforming your reality.

This transformation happens when you bring your considerable will, intent, and desire to bear against whatever it is that you want to change. When the energy of this moon is focused and backed with passion, this change occurs at the quantum level and can result in the remission of illness or disease, sudden rise in wealth and fame, an explosion of psychic ability ... well, you get the general idea.

Scorpio is also about power—the power we wield over others and the power others wield over us. All too often this lunar energy is misused or abused when it concerns power issues; then its tremendous capacity for positive transformation becomes negative. The difference seems to be self-awareness.

It's a great day to work with healing energies, intuitive and psychic development, and research and investigation.

Sagittarius Moon

Mutable Fire Sign

Oh, baby, let the good times roll! And for the Sagittarian moon, those good times mean music, deep talk, exotic travel, esoteric ideas. Today you're an explorer. Those explorations may take you to the farther ends of the Earth or deep within the mysteries of the universe. In one way or another this moon enables you to search for the higher truth, the larger picture, a more expansive perspective.

You may be more blunt than usual when dealing with people today, particularly when the other guy just doesn't get what seems so obvious to you. Patience and nuance aren't your strong points during this period. The exception to this occurs when you're pursuing something about which you feel passionate, then you have the patience of Mother Teresa and are as detail oriented as a Virgo.

You're called to action today. You would rather do than think about doing. As a mutable sign, you're emotionally adaptable. You have opinions about virtually everything and aren't the least bit hesitant in expressing these opinions. This becomes a problem if you're dogmatic or bombastic about what you believe and try to convert others to your way of thinking. So today strive to nurture patience and optimism.

Capricorn Moon

Cardinal Earth Sign

The moon isn't particularly comfortable in this sign. It chafes at all the rules and restrictions that Capricorn seeks to impose and dislikes all that earthy grounding. However, this moon certainly favors strategy—laying out goals and figuring ways to achieve them. Your physical energy is excellent today and enables you to work long hours to meet a deadline, regardless of whether that deadline is self-imposed (which it often is) or imposed by a boss.

You feel quite independent today and may find yourself outdoors, hiking alone through the wilderness, or at the gym, putting in extra time on the treadmill. Under this lunar influence you push yourself, move the bar higher, and feel a certain determination to carve your niche in the larger world.

Today it's easier to categorize your emotions, to look at things dispassionately. So tackle stuff that pushes your buttons, issues that you've pushed aside but which beg for a resolution.

Aquarius Moon

Fixed Air Sign

Today you march to a different drummer. You may hear a different kind of music in your very cells and feel compelled to decipher the message and act on it.

This is the sign, after all, that ushers in new paradigms by refusing to go along with the status quo.

The visionary component to this moon sign gives you an edge today on new trends. You can spot the next wave long before anyone else does. The trick is acting on it and putting it to work for you in your personal and professional life. Your rational mind may try to intervene, to argue and put up blocks, to keep you within the confining box of consensus reality. Or someone close to you—a parent, close friend, significant other—inadvertently plays that role, and you suddenly find yourself on the defensive.

So today be fearless; go forward secure in the knowledge that your vision is correct!

Pisces Moon

Mutable Water Sign

Today you're the archetypal dreamer, your feet never really firmly rooted on the earth. You're deeply compassionate today too, a true bleeding heart. You probably won't be able to pass a homeless person on the street without giving him money, and you definitely won't resist the soulful gaze of a stray pup or kitten. Injustices of any sort may fill you with a deep sadness. Your challenge during this moon is to detach emotionally from situations and people who cause you this kind of anguish.

Part of the problem is that today you're a psychic sponge who soaks up the emotions and moods of the people around you. This alone makes it vital that you associate with upbeat, positive people and situations that boost your energy rather than sap it.

The Pisces moon favors imagination, intuition, and any artistic endeavor. On a strictly mundane level it's a fine day to shop for new clothes, get a new hairdo, or redesign yourself in some way. Also, your dreams should be especially vivid and could contain important insights and information.

Eclipses

Every year there are at least four eclipses—two solar, two lunar. Solar eclipses are like double new moons; the opportunities are twice as powerful and delicious. They usually involve external events. Lunar eclipses are about internal events and emotions. Eclipses always come in pairs and form an axis of energy. If there's a solar eclipse in Aries, for example, about two weeks later there will be a lunar eclipse in Libra, the opposite sign of Aries.

When an eclipse falls in your sun, moon, or rising sign, you will feel the effects quite powerfully. Be sure to check out the Big Picture chapter for your sign, where we talk about the year's eclipses.

CHAPTER 6

Mars in 2014

Mars rules fire sign Aries and corules Scorpio. It takes two years to circle the zodiac and spends about two months in a sign. Think of this planet as the action hero of the zodiac, the one who is always on the move, doing, acting, getting things done, your personal warrior.

The sign and house placement for your natal Mars describes how you use your physical energy, your desire for personal achievement, and the nature of your sexuality. First check out one of the astrology sites listed in the book and find out the sign and house placement for your natal Mars. Then find your natal Mars in the descriptions below.

Mars in Aries or in the First House

Since Mars rules this sign, the planet is happy here and functions at optimum levels. If your natal Mars is in Aries, you go after what you want; you are impulsive, sometimes reckless, and basically fearless. You're the one who loves the roller coasters at theme parks and hikes to the summit of Mount Everest and heads out for parts unknown with just a backpack and an ATM card.

You have a need to dominate your immediate environment, and your leadership ability is strong. But sometimes you may lack direction. You're terrific at initiating projects, but if you lose interest, you walk away without regret and leave what you started for someone else to complete.

Your sex drive is particularly strong and can sometimes manifest selfishly, with little regard for your partner. You could be somewhat accident prone.

Mars in Taurus or in the Second House

You aren't easily discouraged by obstacles of any kind. Your sheer determination and strength of will are well developed, but you may not use these attributes to their fullest. You take practical, purposeful action in everything you begin.

You pursue your financial goals with relentless energy and drive, but you may have trouble holding on to what you earn because you enjoy spending. Try to pay cash for your purchases so that you have a clearer grasp of how much money goes out.

Your sexual nature is sensuous, often passionate. You find pleasure through your profession.

Mars in Gemini or in the Third House

Your energy is expressed mentally and intellectually. You're an avid student—even once you're out of school. You tend to take on multiple projects simultaneously, which scatters your energy. Your mental restlessness needs a creative outlet, otherwise you can become argumentative.

You think well on your feet and make decisions quickly. Sometimes you can be so aggressive about communicating your ideas that you create unnecessary tension. With this placement there can be a lot of competition with siblings. Your challenge is to think before you speak. You pursue your goals well, but sometimes have so many goals that your energy is all over the place.

In terms of sexuality your mind has to be courted and seduced first!

Mars in Cancer or in the Fourth House

Your family life is active and emphasizes the development of individuality, competition, and independence. If you feel you have to dominate the domestic scene, that can sometimes be a source of tension.

Your experiences are filtered through a subjective lens. You may be the kind of person who takes everything personally, so it's difficult at times to be objective about issues that are important to you.

The intuitive component with this placement may give you an advantage in terms of your family. You simply have to tune in to find out what your kids are really doing! This intuitive connection also operates with your partner, parents, and anyone else who shares your domestic life.

Your sexuality is particularly heightened when you're emotionally in synch with your partner.

Mars in Leo or in the Fifth House

You're all about passion. It rushes through everything you do and say, even in the way you move. You have strong leadership abilities, are as fearless as Mars in Aries, and your will is powerful and determined. Artistic or musical skills are sometimes indicated with this placement.

You may be into competitive sports, enjoy strenuous physical activity, and are an ardent and considerate lover. You pursue romance and creative endeavors with equal passion, and with both the one thing you should be careful about is acting impulsively.

Your sexuality is powerful, and others pick up on that, so you have no shortage of people clamoring for your attention.

Mars in Virgo or in the Sixth House

Your energy finds expression through efficient, practical pursuits. You're one of the hardest workers around, especially when the work involves attention to details. You dislike laziness in others and may criticize them for it, but that usually gets you nowhere and doesn't change anything.

You pursue your goals with a quiet diligence, rarely giving up or surrendering to despair when something doesn't work out. Sooner or later you attain what you want.

In terms of sexuality you're quite discriminating and picky about what you want in a partner. But once you're smitten, you tend to be loyal.

Mars in Libra or in the Seventh House

Your energy finds its best expression in partnerships and through and with other people. Your marriage and partnerships are infused with energy and are a source of inspiration to you.

You can charm your way into any situation or relationship. You usually understand another person's point of view because you can put yourself in his or her shoes. You excel at diplomacy and seek harmony and peace in whatever you do.

Your sexuality is determined to a large extent on how romantic you feel. It's about *mood*—how your partner approaches you, talks to you, courts you.

Mars in Scorpio or in the Eighth House

Mars corules Scorpio, so the planet is happy here and functions well. Your drive and ambition are legendary among the people who know you. Even strangers notice something about you that's different, out of the ordinary. Your sexuality is important to you, and the intensity with which it's expressed can be intimidating to others.

This same intensity, however, makes you an excellent investigator and researcher. You're never satisfied with easy answers. You dig and dig, always looking for the absolute bottom line in everything you do.

In a marriage or partnership you're actively involved in joint finances. This could cause friction between you and your partner, but it's something you insist on.

This placement for Mars can be quite psychic. At the very least you may delve into metaphysics, experience past-life recall, or see things that others don't.

Mars in Sagittarius or in the Ninth House

Your energy is best expressed in competitive sports, travel, and adventure, and the study of different cultures, philosophies, and spiritual traditions. Mars in Sagittarius can denote a career in publishing or higher education or as a crusader, a New Age leader, or even as an evangelist. You have the courage to act on your convictions.

Your sexuality is passionate but impulsive. You can commit to a relationship, but only when your heart is truly captured. Otherwise you prefer to remain free and unfettered.

Mars in the ninth house often takes wanderlust to new levels. It isn't enough for you to take an annual vacation. You live to travel, explore, and delve into various philosophies and spiritual traditions first hand.

Mars in Capricorn or in the Tenth House

Your energy finds its best expression in your career and profession. You're a worker who sets goals and moves toward them with a strategy, a plan. You're organized and use your time efficiently. When you want something, nothing holds you back. You pursue it with a self-motivation that others find intimidating and remarkable.

You may keep a tight hold on your sexuality. You're guarded and cautious and may get involved with people who are older than you. You have to be deeply certain about a relationship before you commit fully to it.

As a workaholic, it's smart to kick back sometimes

and evaluate where you are and where you're going. You need down times, periods when you relax and recharge.

Mars in Aquarius or in the Eleventh House

Your energy is best expressed through honing your individuality. You participate in groups when those groups support your interests and passions, but otherwise you're a paragon of individuality. Sometimes your approach is so different from the mainstream that others think you're eccentric.

Mars in the eleventh house explores group participation in a deeper way than Mars in other houses. You take the initiative in forming friendships and joining groups, but always there's a purpose behind it. You excel at initiating projects and launching them.

Your sexuality is apt to be unemotional unless you're madly in love with your partner. That said, love and sex begin in the mind for you.

Mars in Pisces or in the Twelfth House

Your energy is primarily intuitive and emotional. You can be inconsistent in the way you try to achieve your goals, or you're able to intuitively pull together facets of a project and make them work.

Your sexuality is intimately tied to your emotions and intuition. The other person has to "feel" right to you; there has to be some sort of heart-centered connection. With Mars in the twelfth house there can be secrecy surrounding your sexuality and relationships.

Sometimes with this placement there's a need to

recognize the ways in which you are aggressive so that the aggression doesn't turn against you and create health problems.

Important Mars and Venus Combinations

If you have a copy of your birth chart, take a look at where both Mars and Venus are located. If they are in the same sign and house, it suggests your sexuality is central to your life. Your passionate nature propels you into many different types of relationships, and not all of them are positive.

Generally this combination indicates that you're extremely attractive to the opposite sex, are fortunate in financial matters, and have artistic ability. It means your passion can be poured into artistic endeavors.

If your natal Mars is three signs away from your natal Venus (Mars in Aries, Venus in Capricorn, for instance), you may find yourself in stormy romances, where you and your partner are rarely on the same page. You may use other people for sexual gratification—or you're used in this way. That's the worst case scenario. However, with a bit of temperance and balance added to the mix, this combination can lead to a relationship in which you maintain your independence, and you and your partner appreciate each other's differences.

When your natal Mars is two signs away from Venus (Mars in Taurus, Venus in Cancer) or four signs away (Mars in Taurus, Venus in Virgo), you get along very well with the opposite sex. Your romantic relationships, partnerships, and marriage are harmonious and satisfying. A lot of your energy goes into creative pursuits.

If your natal Mars is opposite Venus, romantic and sexual relationships can be difficult. You may have to deal with jealousy and other such dark feelings. Your aggression can be intimidating. In extreme cases there can be abuse in relationships.

Everything in your natal chart, however, is indicative only of potential. What you do with that potential is entirely up to you—and your free will.

CHAPTER 7

The Luck Factor in 2014—Synchronicity

The word *synchronicity* was coined by Swiss psychiatrist Carl Jung, when he wrote the introduction to the Richard Wilhelm translation of the *I Ching*. In a nutshell synchronicity is a meaningful coincidence. It happens when inner and outer events come together in a way that is meaningful to the observer and can't be explained by cause and effect.

We've all experienced these events. You're thinking of a friend you haven't seen for years, and suddenly you get an invite from that person on Facebook. Or you're delayed on your way to work one morning, and when you finally arrive at your turnoff discover there was an accident at just about the time you would have driven through if you'd been on time.

Once you're aware that these incidents hold a deeper meaning, they tend to happen more frequently. As you begin to work with these synchronicities, deciphering their messages, you suddenly realize you're in the flow, in the right place at the right time.

The planet that can help us get into the flow—Jupiter—is also the planet that represents luck and expansion, success, prosperity, growth, creativity, spiritual interests, higher education, and the law. It governs publishing, overseas travel, and foreign countries and any of our dealings with them. This year it will be moving through two signs. Between January 1 and July 16 it will be transiting water sign Cancer. Between July 16 and August 11, 2015, it will be moving through fire sign Leo.

Check out www.synchrosecrets.com for a description of the most common types of synchronicities and how to decipher the messages. Sometimes the messages are obvious. But some synchronicities require interpretation. You have to think symbolically.

Now let's take a look at how these transits might attract more synchronicity and luck into your life.

Aries

If you aren't aware of synchronicity, your best time this year for delving into this fascinating phenomenon is between July 16 and August 11, 2015, when Jupiter transits fellow fire sign Leo, your solar fifth house of love, romance, and creativity.

Consider keeping a journal about your experiences as the synchronicities occur. Or create a file on your computer or iPad. Note what types of synchronicity they are. Do they occur in clusters, with the same name, word, or phrase happening repeatedly during a relatively short period of time? Do your experiences act as guidance, confirmation, warning?

It's easy for you to get into the flow, Aries. Just follow your impulses. They often lead you to exactly where you need to be. Or if you have a hunch that you should follow a particular course, by all means follow the hunch. If a dream provides what seems to be information about an issue that concerns you, be sure to consider this information before making a decision.

Jupiter's transit through Leo indicates that you're going to enjoy delving into the topic of synchronicity and that you and a romantic partner may undertake the exploration together. You should experience luck with your creative endeavors, with projects and opportunities coming to you seemingly out of the blue.

Between January 1 and July 16, when Jupiter is transiting Cancer, your luck is heightened when you use your intuition and may involve your home and domestic environment. You might be able to move into a larger home in a neighborhood that suits your family better. Your family might expand—a birth, a parent or relative moves in, a child moves back home. At each step of the way synchronicities may be happening, particularly if major life transitions are occurring.

Taurus

Your luck factor and your synchronicities should be strongest during Jupiter's transit through compatible water sign Cancer: January 1 to July 16. This transit occurs in your solar third house—your neighborhood/community, siblings and other relatives, education and short-distance travel. These areas of your life may seem particularly lucky, and synchronicities may revolve around these areas.

Since the third house also governs your conscious mind and communication abilities, you may be writing or blogging about your experiences. You might start a Web site or write a book about these experiences.

Consider keeping a journal about your experiences as the synchronicities occur. Or create a file on your computer or iPad. Note what types of synchronicity they are. Do they occur in clusters, with the same name, word, or phrase happening repeatedly during a relatively short period of time? Do your experiences act as guidance, confirmation, warning?

During Jupiter's transit through Leo between July 16, 2014, and August 11, 2015, your luck factor revolves around your home and domestic situation. If you're going through a major transition of some kind—a move, the birth of a child, a change in income—the synchronicities may come fast and furiously.

Gemini

Jupiter's transit through Leo will be the one that is most beneficial for you, your luck factor, and your experience of synchronicity. The dates again: July 16, 2014, to August 11, 2015. It occurs in your solar third house—your neighborhood/community, siblings and other relatives, education and short-distance travel. These areas of your life may seem particularly lucky, and synchronicities may revolve around these areas.

Since the third house also governs your conscious mind and communication abilities, you may be writing or blogging about your experiences. You might start a Web site or write a book about these experiences.

Consider keeping a journal about your experiences as the synchronicities occur. Or create a file on your computer or iPad. Note what types of synchronicity they are. Do they occur in clusters, with the same name, word, or phrase happening repeatedly during a relatively short period of time? Do your experiences act as guidance, confirmation, warning?

Jupiter's transit through Cancer between January 1 to July 16 occurs in your financial area. Expect your financial opportunities to expand tremendously. Your luck factor will revolve around money. Synchronicities will occur in areas where you need guidance, confirmation, or warning.

Cancer

Oh, lucky you! The Jupiter transit to anticipate occurs between January 1 and July 16, when the planet of expansion and luck transits your sign! Everything in your life should expand during this period. Opportunities drop in your lap, your finances probably improve, or you get married or start a new career or family. Your intuition is greatly enhanced during this transit, and you're able to create a rich psychic environment for synchronicity. Be sure to decipher the messages of these synchronicities; they hold valuable information for you.

Consider keeping a journal about your experiences as the synchros occur. Or create a file on your computer or iPad. Note what types of synchronicity they are. Do they occur in clusters, with the same name, word, or phrase happening repeatedly during a relatively short period of time? Do your experiences act as guidance, confirmation, warning?

The second Jupiter transit, through Leo, occurs in

your financial area. This is when your finances really benefit. You land a fat raise, find a new, better-paying job, get a hefty bonus, or pick the right stocks. Synchronicities during this period may revolve around money.

Leo

The first Jupiter transit this year, in Cancer, occurs in your solar twelfth house. The dates: January 1 to July 16.

This period brings heightened insights concerning your own psyche and unconscious. You may try therapy or take up meditation. Jupiter's transit through Cancer makes your unconscious more accessible to you in some way, and you discuss the process with others through a blog or Web site, by writing a book, or keeping a journal. You may even work this process into your professional life in some way. One purpose for this transit is to clear out the old to make way for the new when Jupiter enters your sign on July 16. You may be discarding beliefs that no longer serve your best interests or breaking longstanding habits. Relationships may end but new ones begin.

If you feel this is a period of major transitions for you, the synchronicities are likely to come fast and furiously, offering confirmation, warning, peeks at the future. You might, for instance, dream of someone you know you've never met—only to meet that same person the next day or a week later. Any seeds you sow during this transit will be beneficial down the line, Leo.

During the second transit, when Jupiter is in your

sign, everything in your life opens up. Your luck factor is at its highest, and synchronicities swirl so quickly through your life that you better have a way to record them!

Consider keeping a journal about your experiences as the synchronicities occur. Or create a file on your computer or iPad. Note what types of synchronicity they are. Do they occur in clusters, with the same name, word, or phrase happening repeatedly during a relatively short period of time? Do your experiences act as guidance, confirmation, warning?

Virgo

Between January 1 and July 16 your luck factor and synchronicity experiences revolve around friends, groups to which you belong, your network of friends and acquaintances, and how you can achieve your wishes and dreams. Heady stuff, right?

The contacts you make during this period will be valuable and will expand your dreams in some way. The types of synchronicities you experience could involve virtually anything. The universe has a way of knowing what you need—even if you don't! Be sure to decode the messages that come with these synchronicities; they could prove helpful as guidance and confirmation. Your precision and attention to detail during this time should aid you. Your particular mindset lends itself to solving puzzles and mysteries.

During the second Jupiter transit, which lasts about thirteen months, your personal unconscious expands. This period brings heightened insights concerning your own psyche and unconscious. You may try therapy or take up meditation. Jupiter's transit through Leo and your solar twelfth house makes your unconscious more accessible to you in some way. You may discuss the process with others through a blog or Web site, by writing a book, or keeping a journal. You may even work this process into your professional life in some way.

Libra

During the first six months of the year, while Jupiter transits water sign Cancer and the career area of your chart, your professional life expands tremendously. This period should be exciting, with your professional opportunities multiplying almost more quickly than you can keep up with. You'll be lucky professionally—you're the right person at the right time and place, that sort of lucky. You may change jobs or careers, and if you do, it's for a better position and more pay. You could also be promoted or may decide to launch your own business.

Synchronicity will act as your guide, confirm your hunches, provide warnings or caution, or urge you to move full steam ahead. This period will enable you to make significant professional strides.

The second Jupiter transit, through Leo, occurs between July 16, 2014, and August 11, 2015. It happens in the area of your chart that governs friendships, groups, and your wishes and dreams. The contacts you make during this period will be valuable and expand your dreams in some way. The types of synchronicities you experience could involve virtually anything. The universe has a way of knowing what you need—even if you don't! Be sure to decode the messages that come with these synchronicities; they could prove helpful as guidance and confirmation.

Scorpio

During Jupiter's transit through Cancer, your solar ninth house, between January 1 and July 16 your opportunities and luck factor expand considerably.

The ninth house governs your worldview, higher education, publishing, and foreign travel, so expansions are likely to take place in those areas. Your communication opportunities should expand as well. You might sell a book or novel you've written, go to college or graduate school, or sign up for a seminar or workshop on a topic about which you're passionate. If you travel a great deal during this period, don't be surprised if you begin to experience a flurry of synchronicities.

Your spiritual beliefs will expand too. You may sample different religions or spiritual beliefs, launch a spiritual quest, or even travel to far-flung locales in search of spiritual truths. It all depends, Scorpio, on what you're seeking and how sincere you are in your desires.

Between July 16, 2014, and August 11, 2015, Jupiter transits Leo, your career area, and your professional life expands tremendously. This period should be exciting, with your professional opportunities multiplying almost more quickly than you can keep up with. You'll be lucky professionally—you're the right person at the right time and place, that sort of lucky. You may change jobs or careers, and if you do, it's for a better position and more pay. You could also be promoted or may decide to launch your own business. During this year you have many opportunities to show off your talents and skills.

Consider keeping a journal about your experiences as the synchros occur. Or create a file on your computer or iPad. Note what types of synchronicity they are. Do they occur in clusters, with the same name, word, or phrase happening repeatedly during a relatively short period of time? Do your experiences act as guidance, confirmation, warning?

Sagittarius

Since Jupiter rules your sign, its movements impact you quite personally and powerfully. Between January 1 and July 16 it transits Cancer, your solar eighth house. Your partner's income will expand, and you may be delving more deeply into metaphysics. Your intuitive abilities should deepen considerably under this transit. You may be researching and investigating life after death, communication with spirits, haunted houses, or things that go bump in the night. You'll be fortunate with mundane things as well—mortgages, loans, taxes, insurance, all of which falls under the eighth house. Synchronicities swirl in these areas. You're being guided.

The second transit, between July 16, 2014, and August 11, 2015, occurs in Leo, your solar ninth house. The ninth house governs your worldview, higher education, publishing, and foreign travel, so expansions are likely to take place in those areas. Your communication opportunities should expand as well. You might sell a book or novel you've written, go to college or graduate school, or sign up for a seminar or workshop on a topic about which you're passionate. You'll travel a lot during this period and should experience a flurry of synchronicities.

Your spiritual beliefs will expand too. You may sample different religions or spiritual beliefs, launch a spiritual quest, or even travel to far-flung locales on a spiritual quest of some kind.

Capricorn

During the first six months of the year, while Jupiter transits your opposite sign, Cancer, your partnership opportunities expand tremendously, and there's a strong element of luck to both professional and personal partnerships. You could find exactly the right person for a particular job or as a business partner. You and your partner may decide to move in together or get engaged or married. Be alert for synchronicities in every area of your life, and try to interpret the message and follow the guidance these meaningful coincidences provide.

The second Jupiter transit, between July 16, 2014, and August 11, 2015, occurs in Leo, your solar eighth house. The eighth house dynamics are always intriguing. On one side you have mundane issues—taxes, insurance, bank loans and mortgages—and on the other side you have esoteric stuff—hauntings, life after death, communication with the dead. These issues will be focal points for expansion. Synchronicities are likely to abound in these areas.

It should be easier for you to obtain a mortgage

and bank loan, and you will find yourself drawn to explore things that go bump in the night. You may even travel abroad to investigate crop circles or UFO reports. It all depends on how far outside the box your interests extend.

Aquarius

Between January 1 and July 16 Jupiter transits Cancer, your solar sixth house. The strong intuitive component to this transit helps you make better decisions in your daily work life and in regard to the maintenance of your health. You could land a promotion with more responsibility—and a raise that matches that responsibility—or hire more employees for your company. Regardless, a Jupiter transit usually brings expansion of some kind.

Synchronicities are likely to occur if major life transitions are going on—a move, job or career change, a birth or death in the family, a change in income.

Between July 16, 2014, and August 11, 2015, Jupiter transits Leo, your opposite sign. Your partnership opportunities expand tremendously, and there's a strong element of luck to both professional and personal partnerships. You could find exactly the right person for a particular job or as a business partner. You and your partner may decide to move in together or get engaged or married. Be alert for synchronicities in every area of your life, and try to interpret the message and follow the guidance these meaningful coincidences provide.

Pisces

Jupiter's transit through fellow water sign Cancer between January 1 and July 16 occurs in your solar fifth house—romance, love, creativity! You've got the Midas touch now and synchronicity is your middle name. You may feel you're being led into certain creative endeavors. Luck is on your side. Sounds like a recipe for paradise, doesn't it?

Between July 16, 2014, and August 11, 2015, Jupiter transits Leo, your solar sixth house. This thirteen-month transit should expand your daily work routine and the ways in which you maintain your daily health. You might be promoted, be given more responsibility, and be paid well for it. You might change jobs. However the specifics unfold, you're lucky in this area.

Consider keeping a journal about your experiences as the synchronicities occur. Or create a file on your computer or iPad. Note what types of synchronicity they are. Do they occur in clusters, with the same name, word, or phrase happening repeatedly during a relatively short period of time? Do your experiences act as guidance, confirmation, warning?

CHAPTER 8

Retrograde Planets in 2014

Every planet except the sun and moon experience retrograde motion, when the planet, as viewed from Earth, appears to be moving backward. In astrology a retrograde planet is essentially dormant, like a bear in winter. Its energy is repressed, slower, and often mixed up—as when Mercury, the planet of communication and travel, is retrograde.

During retrograde periods we tend to be less spontaneous, are prompted to think before we speak, and often backtrack through issues, situations, and relationships. We look within. The effect of a retrograde is primarily internal, even though there are many external manifestations of the retrograde.

In 2014 every planet turns retrograde, so let's take a look at when these retrogrades occur and what the effects might be for us.

Mercury

We talk quite a bit throughout the book about Mercury retrograde. It occurs three times a year, for two to three weeks. If you look at the Big Picture chapter for your sign, you'll find a lengthy discussion of Mercury retrograde and what it means for you. So here we're talking generally.

First, Mercury rules both Gemini and Virgo, so the retrogrades may have more of an impact on those two signs. When Mercury turns retrograde, your travel plans go south, there are communication snafus, you miss appointments—or discover you were never on the calendar! If you sign a contract during a Mercury retrograde, the contract may not pan out the way you hoped or the project may fall apart altogether.

In the 2000 presidential election Mercury was retrograde as the election results began to come in. Tom Brokaw announced that Al Gore had won Florida, a critical state for him, and that meant Gore had won the election. But minutes after Mercury turned direct, Brokaw said it was too early to call a winner. Ballot issues were being reported in Palm Beach County. Well, we all know where this one went—straight to the Supreme Court.

Writing now, in early 2012, it looks as if the presidential election is going to have similar issues. On November 6, the day of the election, Mercury turns retrograde in Sagittarius and doesn't turn direct again until November 26. As you read this now in late 2013 or in 2014, you already know how that election turned out!

On a personal level a Mercury retrograde impacts your life according to the sign and natal house in which it falls. Be sure to consult your natal chart as you read through the dates:

February 6 to February 28—retrograde in Pisces. Because it occurs in the early degrees of the sign, Mercury moves back into Aquarius, where it will be when Mercury turns direct again. This means that two areas of your life are affected.

June 7 to July 1—retrograde in Cancer. Again, because it occurs in the early degrees of Cancer, it moves back into Gemini, so two areas of your life are impacted.

October 4 to October 25—retrograde in Scorpio. It begins in the early degrees of Scorpio, slides back into Libra, so once again two areas of your life are affected.

Venus

Venus rules both Taurus and Libra, so they may feel the impact of a Venus retrograde more strongly than other signs. It turns retrograde once every eighteen months or so, and the retrograde period last about six weeks.

When Venus turns retrograde, your love life and finances are often impacted. Relationship issues resurface, and former lovers and spouses may suddenly appear. Friends you haven't heard from in years may get in touch out of the blue. It's an excellent time to reevaluate your closest relationships and decide what you're looking for in a partner.

If you're in a committed relationship, you and your

partner may be sifting back through issues that you thought had been resolved. One or both of you may be distant, emotionally absent, during the retrograde period.

In terms of finances your expenses may increase, and you could feel pinched. The sign and house where Venus falls during the retrograde is important, so be sure to check your natal chart. It's important to avoid buying large-ticket items. That said, however, it's possible to find great deals during a Venus retrograde. One year we bought a used car during a Venus retrograde, only to discover it had been in an accident before we'd bought it. We took it back to the company that sold us the car, and they fixed the problem. We then sold it a year later—for the same price we'd paid for it.

In 2014 Venus is retrograde between January 1 and 31 in Capricorn, a continuation of a retrograde that began in December 2013. Between January 1 and 11 Mercury is traveling with retrograde Venus, which suggests that your focus is strongly on career and professional matters, and you could be discussing things because of some rough patches.

Mars

Mars rules Aries and corules Scorpio, so these two signs may feel the impact of a Mars retrograde most strongly. A Mars retrograde occurs every two years and two months and lasts between fifty-eight to eighty-one days. In 2014 Mars begins the year retrograde in Libra, and that continues until March 1.

During a Mars retrograde your physical energy may not be up to par, so if you're partying every night, not getting enough sleep, pushing against a deadline, eating on the run . . . you may get run down. In other words, take extra good care of yourself during this period.

Mars rules our capacity for physical aggression, how we pursue our ambitions, our sexuality. The retrograde period can prompt you to bottle up anger, which can be detrimental on several levels: the anger festers and then explodes, or it festers and your blood pressure rises, or you get sick. Anger consumes enormous amounts of energy, so you end up feeling exhausted and depressed.

If you're angry at someone in particular, write the person a letter and review every word to make sure you've said exactly what you want to say. Then make a decision about whether to hold onto the letter until Mars turns direct or to give it to the person. Sometimes just writing out what you're feeling defuses the anger.

In terms of your professional life and career, projects and connections may be delayed, don't happen quickly enough, or fall apart midway through the process.

One of the best ways to deal with a Mars retrograde is through physical activity. Be sure to keep up your exercise routine. Or try new forms of exercise — yoga, pilates, brisk walking, running, or playing sports.

Jupiter

Jupiter rules Sagittarius and corules Pisces, so these two signs are apt to feel a Jupiter retrograde more strongly. Jupiter rules travel, luck, speculation, optimism, worldview, philosophy, religion, higher education, and expansion.

For about four months every year it turns retrograde. During this period you're more likely to look within for answers, and it's possible to attain a new level of awareness. You may question issues like self-worth and could be redefining yourself and your values in some way. As your worldview and spiritual beliefs expand, your external life eventually does too.

During a Jupiter retrograde meditation can be enormously beneficial. You're able to center yourself and turn within to find the answers and insights that benefit you. Take a workshop or seminar in intuitive development during the retrograde. Listen to affirmation and visualization tapes.

In 2014 there are two periods when Jupiter is retrograde. Between January 1 and March 6 it's retrograde in Cancer, a continuation of a retrograde that began in November 2013. Then on July 16 Jupiter enters Leo and turns retrograde on December 8. This retrograde lasts until April 8, 2015. Find out where Cancer and Leo fall in your natal chart; those are the areas where the retrograde will affect you most strongly.

Saturn

Saturn rules Capricorn, so when it's retrograde Capricorns are likely to feel the impact strongly. The planet turns retrograde about once a year and remains that way for about four and a half months.

Saturn rules responsibility, obligation, structure, limitations, delays, authority, conservatives, and karma. During the retrograde period everything seems to slow down. You learn how to push through self-imposed limitations because you now have the time to do so. Projects you thought were done deals may be delayed. It's wise not to try to rush things during this retrograde. Strive for what's practical and efficient.

Saturn's energy, direct or retrograde, is difficult to navigate at times. But one way or another we all manage to do so. Keep that in mind during the 2014 retrograde between January 1 and March 6, a continuation of a retrograde that began in 2013. Saturn will be retrograde in Scorpio then, so everything you encounter is likely to have an intense, bottom-line feel to it. Just try to go with the flow, and don't offer resistance!

Uranus

Uranus rules Aquarius, our individuality, sudden, unexpected change, genius, electronics, rebellion, freedom, and revolution. It turns retrograde once a year for about five months.

This planet's job is to awaken us with sudden, unexpected, and jolting events that prompt us to change the things in our lives that no longer work in our best interests. When it's retrograde, you may rebel against the status quo, whatever that is for you, and seek to free yourself from restrictive situations and relationships. You may experience sudden flashes of insight about a concern you have or that illuminates a creative endeavor in which you're involved.

Be sure to check out where Uranus is located in your natal chart. As Uranus retrogrades, you will feel it most strongly when it forms an angle to your natal Uranus or to another planet in your chart.

In 2014 Uranus in Aries is retrograde between July 21 and December 21.

Neptune

Neptune rules Pisces, higher inspiration, illusions, escapism, addiction, creativity, and spirituality. Once a year it's retrograde for about five months.

During this period your inspiration is likely to be powerful, and you'll be able to draw on deep, inner resources for any creative endeavors. Your spiritual beliefs may change or deepen, and you may spend a lot of time reading and studying about various spiritual traditions. It's an excellent period for dream work. Your dreams provide insights, information, and inspiration.

Note where Neptune is in your natal chart, and pay attention to when transiting Neptune is going to form an angle to it or to another natal planet. Neptune often blurs the boundaries between you and other people, so you may have to reestablish those boundaries.

In 2014 Neptune is retrograde in Pisces between June 9 and November 15.

Pluto

Pluto moves at a snail's pace and takes 250 years to circle the zodiac. It rules Scorpio, transformation, human evolution, and everything that is hidden and unseen. In 2014 its retrograde period is from April 14 to September 22.

During this period you have the opportunity to dive into yourself and figure out what's most important to you. Sometimes retrograde periods bring about personal loss and events that are beyond your control. That's how Pluto forces us to evolve and grow, to transform.

If you don't meditate already, start doing it before Pluto turns retrograde. That way the retrograde period may be less jarring for you, and regardless of what happens you'll remain centered and grounded.

Keep Track of Your Retrograde Experiences

During the retrograde of each of the planets this year, keep a record of what you experience. By doing this you build up knowledge about you as impacted by retrograde.

CHAPTER 9

Health Tips for 2014

Why You Take Responsibility

Statistics can be real eye openers. We recently ran across some facts related to health care in the U.S. And they are sobering.

More money per person is spent on health care in the United States than in any other country in the world. Yet life expectancy in this country ranks fiftieth, and the U.S. lags behind other wealthy nations in infant mortality. According to the Institute of Medicine, the United States is the only country in the world that doesn't ensure that all its citizens have health coverage.

When Obama signed the Affordable Care Act into law in 2010, the politically conservative faction screamed that it was socialism. It's not. Socialized medicine is full coverage by the *government*. The mandate in the U.S. was a triumph for private insurance companies, whose bottom line is profit, not health. They will now gain nearly 50 million new clients.

In all fairness, there are some good things about this mandate. Children can be on their parents' insurance policies until the age of twenty-six, and no one can be denied health insurance because of a preexisting condition. Not surprisingly, the mandate has been challenged in court and will come before the Supreme Court in March 2011. You, reading this in 2014, already know the outcome. We don't.

One of the most famous moments in the health care debacle was when an older woman at a Tea Party meeting waved her sign—*No to Obama Care*—while she shouted, "Keep your hands off my Medicare!"

You know, Medicare, the *government-run* insurance program for people sixty-five and older. Medicare for all should have been implemented, not mandated by health insurance.

Until insurance companies are removed from health care, the health care in this country will continue to be a discriminatory system. The real death panels will continue to be insurance companies who deny care for profit.

If nothing else, that debate and the reality of health care in this country should encourage you to take charge of your own health. Here are some simple suggestions:

1) *If you don't have a regular exercise routine yet, start one.* Pick something that you know you can do daily.

2) *Watch what you eat. Read the labels on the food you buy.* How much sodium is there in your favorite foods? How much cholesterol? Fats? Even organic foods have a high sodium content. The other day at Whole Foods we picked up some soy bacon and then

turned the box over to look at the contents. For a single slice of soy bacon, the nutritional facts state:

Total fat—1 gram
No saturated or trans fat, no polyunsaturated or monounsaturated fats
Cholesterol—0 mg
Sodium—140 mg
Potassium—40 mg
No carbs, no sugar
Protein—2 g

That's a lot of sodium for a single skinny slice of soy bacon! Compare this to our favorite organic chicken sausage, however, which has 460 mg of sodium for a single link, and the soy bacon looks good. Once you get into the habit of reading the labels, you will be more careful in your selection of foods.

3) *Meditation and yoga are two healthy practices you might consider.* Meditation has been shown to: lower blood pressure and oxygen consumption, decrease respiratory rate, slow heart rate, reduce anxiety and stress, and enhance the immune system. Yoga increases your physical flexibility—and eventually your emotional and mental flexibility as well. It helps to strengthen your body, improves muscle tone, improves posture, improves lung capacity because of the deep breathing involved, and reduces stress.

4) *Try various nutritional and vitamin programs.* Educate yourself. The Internet is filled with health and fitness Web sites.

5) *Try a homeopathic practitioner or acupuncturist before you run to your doctor for a prescription.*

If you were an alien watching the evening news and the drug commercials that sponsor it, you might get the impression that Americans are a sickly lot in search of the quickest fix. While drugs certainly have their place, more and more Americans are seeking alternative treatments for whatever ails them. From acupuncture to yoga and homeopathy, from vitamin regimens to nutritional programs, more of us are taking control over our own health and bodies.

6) *Take inventory of your beliefs*. If medical intuitives like Louise Hay, Carolyn Myss, and Mona Lisa Schultz are correct, our health is about more than just eating right and getting sufficient exercise. It's also about our emotions, inner worlds, and belief systems. How happy are you in your job? Your closest partnerships? Your friendships? Are you generally happy with the money you earn? What would you change about your life? Do you believe you have free will or that everything is destined? Is your mood generally upbeat? Do you feel you have choices? Do you feel empowered? By asking yourself these kinds of questions, you can glean a sense of your emotional state at any given time. And the state of your emotions may tell you a great deal about the state of your health.

7) *Forgive yourself and others*. Resentment that you keep bottled up inside you for months or even years can adversely affect your health. It's why medical intuitives and holistic physicians recommend practicing the art of forgiveness. It's not easy to forgive people who have hurt you, but once you're able to forgive them, you're releasing resentment.

8) *Practice the art of appreciation. Expect the best from others*. If you can get into the habit of doing

these two things, you're well ahead of the game in maintaining your health.

The Physical You

These descriptions fit both sun and rising signs. For a more complete look at the physical you, of course, your entire natal chart should be taken into account, with a particularly close look at the sign of your moon—the root of your emotions, the cradle of your inner world.

Aries

Rules: Head and Face

2014 Tip:

In this year of the new you try something new in the way you care for yourself and your health.

Health and Fitness

Aries rules the head and face, so these areas are often the most vulnerable physically. Headaches, dizziness, and skin eruptions can be common. If you're an athletic Aries, do more of whatever it is that you enjoy. Competitive sports? Great, go for it. Long distance runner? Run farther. Gym? Double your time and your workout. Yoga once a week? Do it three times a week. One way or another, you need to burn off your excessive energy so that it doesn't turn inward and short-circuit your body!

As a cardinal fire sign, you're an active person who gravitates toward daring, risky sports—mountain climbing, rappelling, bungee jumping, trekking through high mountainous regions, leaping out of airplanes. It's probably a great idea to have good health insurance or to have a Louise Hay attitude toward your health—*I'm attracting only magnificent experiences into my life.*

For maximum benefit, you probably should try to eliminate red meat from your diet. Chicken and fish are fine, but a vegan diet would be best. Herbs like mustard, eye-bright, and bay are beneficial for you. Any antioxidant is helpful—particularly vitamins C, E, A, or Lutein for your eyes, zinc, Co-Q10, Black Cohosh if you're a female in menopause, or Saw Palmetto if you're a man older than fifty. If you pull a muscle or throw your back out of whack, look for a good acupuncturist and avoid pain killers.

In this year of the new you, practice what you learned last year to transform yourself from the inside out. Start with your thoughts. Notice what you think throughout a given day. If you notice that a lot of negative thoughts surface, nudge them on their way by reaching for more positive ones.

Taurus

Rules: Neck, Throat, Cervical Vertebrae

2014 Tip:

In this year of the new you, reach out to strangers, join a group of like-minded individuals, and keep expressing your feelings. Blogging is one excellent way to do that.

Health and Fitness

Thanks to the sensuality of your sign, you may be a gourmet cook and enjoy rich foods. But because your metabolism may be somewhat slow, you benefit from daily exercise and moderation in your diet. In fact, moderation in all things is probably a good rule to follow.

As a fixed earth sign, you benefit from any outdoor activity, and the more physical it is, the better it is for you. Hiking, skiing, windsurfing, biking are all excellent pursuits. You also benefit from any mind/body discipline like tai chi or yoga. The latter is especially good since it keeps you flexible, and that flexibility spills over into your attitudes and beliefs and the way you deal with situations and people. You probably enjoy puttering in a garden, but because you have such an artistic side, you don't just putter. You remake the garden into a work of art—fountains, bold colors, mysterious paths that twist through greenery and flowers. Once you add wind chimes and bird feeders, nature's music adds the finishing touches.

If your job entails long hours of sitting in front of a computer, your neck and shoulders may be more tense than usual. You would benefit through regular massage and hot tub soaks.

If you're the silent type of Taurus, then chances are you don't discuss your emotions. This tendency can cause health challenges if you keep anger or resentment bottled up inside you. Best to have an outlet—through exercise, for example, or through some sort of creative endeavor. Art, music, photography, writing—

any of those would help. Better yet, learn to open up with at least one or two people!

Gemini

Rules: Hands, Arms, Lungs, Nervous System

2014 Tip:

In this year of the new you, practice focusing on one thing at a time. Don't spread yourself too thinly.

Health and Fitness

You benefit from periodic breaks in your established routine. Whether it's a trip to some exotic port or a trip to the grocery, it's a breath of fresh air, a way to hit the pause button on your busy mind. Regular physical exercise helps to bleed off some of your energy and keeps your already youthful body supple and in shape.

As a mutable air sign, you need intellectual stimulation and a constant array of experiences and information to keep your curiosity piqued. Otherwise it's too easy for all that nervous energy to turn inward and affect your health. The kind of work you do is important in the overall scheme of your health. You do best in nonroutine kinds of work with flexible hours or, preferably, in a profession where you make your own hours! Any job in communication, travel, public relations, would suit you. When you're passionate about what you do, you're happier. If you're happy, your immune system remains healthy.

With your natural dexterity and coordination, you

would do well at yoga. If you don't take classes yet, sign up for some. Not only will they keep you flexible, but you'll benefit mentally. Meditation would also be an excellent practice for you. Anything to calm your busy head!

Since your respiratory and nervous systems are your most vulnerable areas, your diet should include plenty of fish, fresh fruits, and vegetables. If you live in a place where you can garden, then plant some of these items in a garden for optimum freshness. Vitamin C, zinc, the B vitamins, and vitamins E and A are also beneficial for you. With your energy always in fast-forward, it's smart to get at least seven and preferably eight hours of sleep a night. If you're the type of Gemini with a high metabolism, you benefit from eating several small meals throughout the day rather than just the usual three.

Cancer

Rules: Breasts, Stomach, Digestive System

2014 Tip:

During this year of the new you, practice being more objective.

Health and Fitness

As a cardinal water sign, you benefit from proximity to water. If you can live or work close to a body of water, you'll notice a marked difference in your energy and intuition and how you feel and think. Even a vacation close to it is healing. This seems to hold true not only for Cancer sun signs, but for moon and rising signs in Cancer too. The body of water can be anything—a lake, river, ocean, salt marsh, even a pond!

Not surprisingly, you benefit from any kind of water sport, even a day at the beach or a picnic by the river. The point is that water speaks to you. It feels like your natural element. You might want to read *The Secret of Water* or any of the other books by Masaru Emoto. You will never think of water in the same way again and will be more conscious of how human emotions affect water—and thus our bodies, since we consist of nearly 70 percent water.

Emotionally you may cling to past injuries and hurts more than other signs or may still be dragging around issues from childhood or even from a past life. Unresolved emotional stuff can lodge in your body and create problems. So it's important that you rid yourself of past resentments and anger. Use hypnosis to dislodge these feelings. Forgive and forget. Have a past-life regression. Read Louise Hay's book *You Can Heal Your Life.*

If you have a moon, rising, or another planet in an earth sign, consider regular workouts at a gym.

Leo

Rules: Heart, Back, Spinal Cord

2014 Tip:

In this year of the new you, keep drama to a minimum. Whenever you feel yourself at the brink of an emotional outburst or meltdown, detach, step back.

Health and Fitness

Leo rules the heart. So you benefit from a low-fat diet, exercise, work that you love, and relationships in which you are recognized as the unique person that you are. Yes, those last two things count in the overall picture of your health!

Let's talk about your work. Acting, of course, is what you're known for. And performance. And politics. And, well, anything where you can show off your abundant talents. So if right now you're locked into a humdrum job, low person on the bureaucratic totem pole, and don't receive the attention you feel you deserve, then your pride and ambition are suffering. That, in turn, creates resentment that could be eating you alive. Turn the situation around by finding a career or an outlet where your talents shine and you're appreciated and recognized. You're a natural leader whose flamboyant style and magnetism attract the supporters who can help you.

You have a temper, but once you blow, that's it. Unlike Cancer, you don't hold on to grudges or harbor resentments or anger from childhood. You tend to be forward looking in your outlook, and your natural optimism is healthy for your heart and immune system. Anything you can do to maintain your cheerful disposition is a plus. When you feel yourself getting down, rent comedies, find books that make you laugh out loud, blog about your feelings.

Virgo

Rules: Intestines, Abdomen, Female Reproductive System

2014 Tip:

Since this is the year of the new you, stick to your exercise routine. Do it regularly. And strive not to be self-critical.

Health and Fitness

If you're the type of Virgo who worries and frets a lot, the first place it's likely to show up is in your digestive tract. You might have had colic as an infant, stomach upsets as a teenager, ulcers as an adult. The best way to mitigate this tendency, of course, is to learn how NOT to worry and to simply go with the flow.

You do best on a diet that includes plenty of fresh fruits and vegetables, fish, and chicken. Try to stay away from fried or heavily spiced foods. Red meat might be difficult to digest. If you live in a place where fresh fruits and vegetables are difficult to find during the winter, supplement your diet with the appropriate vitamins and minerals. If you're a fussy eater—and some Virgos are—the vitamin and mineral supplements are even more important.

You benefit from hot baths, massages, anything that allows you to relax into the moment. Yoga, running, swimming, gym workouts—any of these exercise regimens benefit you. Some Virgos, particularly double Virgos—with a moon or rising in that sign—have an acute sense of smell. If you're one of those, be sure to treat yourself to scented soaps and lotions, fragrant candles and incense, and any other scent that soothes your soul.

Virgo is typically associated with service, and you may find that whenever you do a good deed for someone, when you volunteer your time or expertise, you feel better about yourself and life in general. The more you can do to trigger these feelings, the healthier you'll be. You have a tendency toward self-criticism that's part and parcel of your need for perfection, and whenever you find yourself shifting into that critical frame of mind, stop it in its tracks. Reach for a more uplifting thought. This will help you to maintain your health.

Libra

Rules: Lower Back, Kidney, Diaphragm

2014 Tip:

During this year of the new you, try not to bend over backward to please the people in your life.

Health and Fitness

If your love life is terrific, then your health probably is too. You're happiest when you're in a relationship, preferably a committed, lifetime relationship. When things between you and your partner are on an even keel, your energy is greater, your immune system works without a hitch, you sleep more soundly, and you're more apt to have a healthier lifestyle.

You prefer working in an environment that's aesthetically pleasing, where there's a minimum of drama, and with congenial people. If your work situation doesn't fit that description, it could affect your health—and for the same reason as a love life that is lacking—emotions. Your lower back, kidneys, and diaphragm are vulnerable areas for you and unvented emotions could manifest in those areas first. If it isn't possible to change jobs or careers right now, then find an artistic outlet for your creative expression. Music, photography, art, writing, dance, any area that allows you to flex your creativity.

You benefit from yoga, walking, swimming, and any kind of exercise that strengthen your lower back muscles. Meditation is also beneficial, particularly when it's combined with an awareness of breathing.

The healthiest diet for you should consist of foods with varied tastes, plenty of fresh fruits and vegetables, organic if possible, and a minimum of meats. Anything that benefits your kidneys is good. Drink at least eight glasses of water a day, so that your kidneys are continually flushed out.

Scorpio

Rules: Sexual Organs, Elimination

2014 Tip:

In this year of the new you, listen closely to your intuition, particularly in health matters.

Health and Fitness

As a fixed water sign, you probably benefit by a proximity to water every bit as much as Cancer does. Lake, ocean, river, ocean, pond, salt marsh—take your pick. If none of these is available, put a fountain in your backyard or somewhere in your house, and create a meditation area. It's important that you have a quiet center where you can decompress at the end of the day, particularly if you have a busy family life and a lot of demands on your time.

You tend to keep a lot of emotion locked inside, and if the emotions are negative—resentment, anger—they fester and affect your health. So try to find someone you can talk to freely about your emotions—a partner, friend, family member. Or pour these feelings into a creative outlet. One way or another, get them out.

Scorpio rules the sexual and elimination organs, so these areas could be where ill health hits first. Be sure that you eat plenty of roughage in your diet and enjoy what you eat, while you're eating it. Stay away from the usual culprits—fried or heavily processed foods. You do best with plenty of fresh food, but may want to consider eliminating red meats. Consider colonic treatments for cleaning out the bowels.

For your overall health, it's important to enjoy sex with a partner whom you trust. Avoid using sex as a leverage for power in a relationship.

Sagittarius

Rules: Hips, Thighs, Liver

2014 Tip:

The new you in 2014 is a person who commits to a healthy lifestyle.

Health and Fitness

As a mutable fire sign, you can't tolerate any kind of restriction or limitation on your freedom. You must be able to get up and go whenever you want. If you work in a job that demands you punch a time clock, where your hours are strictly regulated, or are in a relationship where you feel constricted, you probably aren't happy. For a naturally buoyant and happy person like you, that could spell health challenges. Sadge rules the hips, the sacral region of the spine, the coccygeal vertebrae, the femur, the ileum, the iliac arteries, and the sciatic nerves, so any of these areas could be impacted health-wise.

You benefit from any kind of athletic activity. From competitive sports to an exercise regimen you create, your body craves regular activity. You also benefit from yoga, which keeps your spine and hips flexible.

If you're prone to putting on weight—and even if you're not!—strive to minimize sweets and carbs in your diet. The usual recommendations—abundant fresh vegetables and fruits—also apply. If you're the type who eats on the run, you may be eating fast or heavily processed foods and should try to keep that to a minimum or eliminate it altogether. Even though your digestive system is hardy enough to tolerate just about anything, the fast foods and processed foods add carbs and calories.

Antioxidants are beneficial, of course, and these include vitamins C, A, and E. Minerals like zinc should be included in your diet and also a glucosamine supplement for joints.

Capricorn

Rules: Knees, Skin, Bones

2014 Tip:

The new you understands the value of relaxation and doing what you enjoy.

Health and Fitness

Since you seem to have been born with an innate sense of where you're going—or want to go—it's likely that you take care of yourself. You know the routine as well as anyone—eat right, stay fit, exercise, get enough rest. But there are other components to living long and prospering (to paraphrase Spock!). And that's your emotions.

You, like Scorpio, are secretive, although your motives are different. For you it's a privacy factor more than anything else. You keep your emotions to yourself and may not express what you feel when you feel it. This can create blockages in your body, notably in your joints or knees. It's vital that you learn to vent your emotions, to rid yourself of anger before it has a chance to move inward.

You're focused, ambitious, and patient in the attainment of your goals. But your work—your satisfaction with it—is a primary component in your health. If you feel you've reached a dead end in your career, if you're frustrated more often than you're happy with what you do, it's time to revamp and get out of Dodge. By taking clear, definite steps toward something else, you feel you're more in control of your destiny and mitigate the possibility of health challenges.

Since your knees are vulnerable, running is probably not the best form of exercise for you, unless you do it only once or twice a week and engage in some other form of exercise the rest of the time. For a cardio workout that isn't as tough on your knees, try a rowing machine. For general flexibility, there's nothing like yoga!

Aquarius

Rules: Ankles, Shins, Circulatory System

2014 Tip:

In this year of the new you, Aquarius, you maintain your exercise routine. No more cheating!

Health and Fitness

Let's start with the effect of Uranus ruling your sign. It sometimes can set your nerves on edge—too many sounds, too much chaos around you, loud noises deep into the night, the backfiring of cars, the incessant drone of traffic, even a crowd at the local mall. You're sensitive to all of that. It's part of what makes it important for you to have a private space to which you can withdraw—a quiet back yard filled with plants, a room inside your house with an altar for your Wiccan practice, filled with scents from candles or incense that soothe your frazzled nerves. Or perhaps a book on tape can shut it all out. But shut it out you must to protect your health.

Because you live so much inside your own head, exercise is definitely beneficial for you. It doesn't have to be anything complicated—yoga done in the privacy of your own home, long walks, regular bike rides. But do *something* to ground your body, to get your blood moving, to silence the buzz inside your head. It will all benefit your health.

Nutrition? Well for an Aquarian this can go any number of different ways. You enjoy different types of food, so that's a place to start—with what you *enjoy*. The foods are likely to be unusual—organically grown, for instance, prepared in unusual ways, or purchased from a local co-op. If you live in the city, perhaps you purchase food from a grocery store you've been frequenting for years. The idea here is that *you* know what's best for your body, what you can tolerate, what you need. Even though Aquarians aren't generally as in touch with their bodies as earth signs, they have an intuitive sense about what works for them. In the end that's all that matters.

Pisces

Rules: Feet, Lymphatic System

2014 Tip:

The new you treats yourself as you treat others.

Health and Fitness

Let's start with emotions. Let's start with the fact that you're a psychic sponge, able to absorb other people's moods and thoughts with the ease of a magnet attracting every other piece of metal around it. Yes, let's start there. It's why you should associate only with optimistic, upbeat people. The negative types steal your energy, wreck your immune system, and leave you in a tearful mess at the end of the rainbow with nothing to show for your journey.

Like your fellow water signs Cancer and Scorpio, you probably benefit from proximity to water. Whether you live near water, work near it, or vacation near it, water refreshes your soul, spirit, intuition, and immune system. Read Masaru Emoto's books on how water responds to emotions and intent. You'll never think about water in the same way again. You'll never think about your sun sign in the same way again either.

You benefit from any kind of exercise, but try something that speaks to your soul. Swimming. Rowing, but in an actual boat, on an actual river instead of in a gym. Even a hot tub where you kick your legs is beneficial. Pay attention to the water you drink. Is your tap water filled with fluorides? Then avoid it, and look for distilled water. Drink at least eight glasses a day. Indulge yourself in massages, foot reflexology, periodic dips in the ocean. Any ocean.

CHAPTER 10

Your Creativity in 2014

We're innately creative beings who reinvent ourselves constantly. From our appearances to the way we work to our interactions with others, we rarely repeat the same action in exactly the same way. In 2014 it's important that we use our creativity to solve problems and meet challenges in our work, careers, and relationships.

Due to rapidly changing technology, some of us may need to reinvent ourselves professionally. With the popularity of ebooks, for instance, the publishing industry is no longer as centralized as it once was. Writers can now self-publish through any number of services and link their books to Amazon. Artists or photographers who once had to haul around portfolios can now have digital portfolios. Actors and actresses who once had to carry around scripts while learning their lines can now use iPads to view their lines.

How can you use your creativity to redefine yourself this year? Let's take a look.

Aries

As a natural trailblazer and entrepreneur, you have no trouble coming up with new ideas about how to reinvent yourself. Your challenge, though, is carrying through from beginning to end.

The carry-through may be easier for you to accomplish while Jupiter is in fellow fire sign Leo, between July 16, 2014, and August 11, 2015. Jupiter helps you to expand your ideas, to develop your creativity to the point where it becomes second nature. You also have Uranus in your sign helping you to get rid of whatever has gone stale in your life.

So during 2014 don't hesitate to think outside the box, take professional and emotional risks, and follow impulses. It's your path to embracing change.

Taurus

As a fixed earth sign, you are slow to change. You tend to hold on to clothes you no longer wear, jobs that don't suit you, relationships that you've outgrown. In any area where you feel dissatisfaction this year, take a closer look and try to determine if your feelings are transitory, just a mood, or whether it's something more than that. If your dissatisfaction is genuine, how can you change things around?

If your job is the problem, perhaps there are additional skills you can learn and credentials you can garner that will enable you to land a better job that is more suited to your temperament and in a field you love. That's the point here: change that you enjoy, that helps you to evolve creatively.

Develop a strategy, and then use your resoluteness to make it work. This process will be easier for you between January 1 and July 16, while Jupiter transits compatible water sign Cancer and expands your intuition.

Gemini

Change is your middle name. Your challenge, though, is that you sometimes change so rapidly that you aren't sure who you are when you get up in the morning. It's why your sign depicts twins!

In 2014 use your adaptability and innate creativity to focus on one particular area in your life that you would like to change—job, career, relationships, finances. Whatever the area is, decide what you want, how you might best attain it, and then pursue it. If you're the kind of Gemini who enjoys writing, consider blogging about your experiences. You never know how it may help or influence someone else.

Your best time for initiating change and using your creativity to bring it about falls between July 16, 2014, and August 11, 2015, when Jupiter transits compatible fire sign Leo. During this period you're on a creative roll.

Cancer

You're usually so in touch with your feelings that you know when dissatisfaction is just a passing mood and when it addresses something deeper. So take that area of your life where you're feeling genuine dissatisfaction and try to see it objectively. That may be a challenge for you, Cancer. You tend to view the world through a subjective lens, but in this instance objectivity will serve you better.

Once you've identified whatever it is you want to change, use your prodigious intuition to figure out how to initiate the change. Use dream recall, meditation, visualization, and the other intuitive tools you possess. Then act on that information, trusting that your guidance will bring about what you desire.

Synchronicities may proliferate during this process, so be sure to decipher the messages, these signs and symbols that lead you through the unknown. This process will be greatly facilitated between January 1 and July 16, when Jupiter transits your sign.

Leo

Like your fixed-sign cousin Taurus, you're not crazy about change. You like things the way they are, thank you very much. Yet when you feel a deep dissatisfaction about something in your life, you certainly have the creative abilities to initiate change and transform your job, relationships, finances, whatever it is.

As Jupiter transits your sign between July 16, 2014, and August 11, 2015, there will be a lot of changes. This planet seeks to expand your life and creative abilities and ushers in the opportunities for doing so. Your challenge will be to avoid drama and just get on with it.

Jupiter's transit through Cancer from January 1 to July 16 will enable you to hone in on beliefs and attitudes that may be holding you back. Once you understand the origin of these beliefs, you can use them as creative fodder, so they are really illuminated to your conscious mind, and change them. Then you can change those beliefs, and your life will change accordingly.

Virgo

You, like your mutable cousin Gemini, welcome change. But you prefer it to occur on your terms, in your time frame, according to your specifications; in other words, when you're ready for it. But because you share the planet with seven billion other souls, change often happens on its own, and then you have to adapt quickly to the new circumstances. You have a plethora of creative talents that enable you to do this.

Your creativity, in fact, is central to who you are. Whether change is something you initiate, or it comes about due to global events, your creativity kicks in, and you're able to move with the flow. Your creativity is apt to be enormously powerful between January 1 and July 15, when Jupiter transits compatible water sign Cancer.

During this transit your intuition expands, and you're able to tap deep creative reservoirs in your being. Don't fritter away this opportunity for personal and professional growth.

Libra

You, like your cardinal cousins Aries and Cancer, are a focused individual and aren't fond of change that is thrust upon you. But when that happens, your creative talents rush in to help you sort things out, and you're able to use the change to your advantage.

If there's some area of your life where you feel dissatisfied, bring your enormous focus to bear on changing it. Don't concentrate on what's wrong, but on the end result you want. See it vividly in your mind—a new you, more money, a better job, a relationship. Whatever it is, imagine it and back that image with emotion.

Your best time for making things happen occurs during Jupiter's transit of compatible fire sign Leo between July 16, 2014, and August 11, 2015.

Scorpio

Your creativity is legendary among the people who know you, and in 2014 it could become legendary to the rest of the world too. You, like your fixed cousins Taurus and Leo, tend to be quite stubborn about how to do something. In 2014 this stubbornness serves you well when it comes to your creative endeavors. You know for an end product, so stick to what you know. However, be open to suggestions by other creative people.

If there are areas of your life that beg for change, shed the stubbornness, delve deeply into your intuitive ability, and figure out what your ideal is. Then listen to your intuition about how to attract the ideal into your life.

This process will be easier when Jupiter is in fellow water sign Cancer between January 1 and July 16.

Sagittarius

You enjoy change, as long as it doesn't restrict your freedom. After all, the source of your creativity is that very freedom you savor, which is as necessary to your life as oxygen.

If there is a particular area of your life that dissatisfies you, it's time to hit the road, Sadge, and allow your creativity to come up with options, solutions, answers, a strategy. Your muse will come out of hiding as soon as you're traveling, and then it's up to you to listen closely, interpret, and create.

Your best time for engaging this process is when Jupiter transits fellow fire sign Leo between July 16, 2014, and August 11, 2015.

Capricorn

You're a focused, self-directed individual who wants life to be grounded, tangible, and unfold one step at a time. You usually know when something in your life is *off,* but may not know how to correct it. That's when your creativity sweeps in and discovers the options, solutions, the new path.

During Jupiter's transit of Cancer, your opposite sign, between January 1 and July 16 your intuition deepens and becomes one of your staunchest allies. A family member or partner—business or romantic—may prove helpful in changing something essential in your life.

The beauty of Capricorn's energy is simple. You steadily climb the mountain toward your goal, and when you encounter a block, you search for and usually find an alternate path to wherever you're going.

Aquarius

You and your fixed-sign cousins—Taurus, Leo, Scorpio—aren't fond of change. But you understand that change is inevitable, that it's the only constant, and so you embrace it as you do most things in life, with your intellect. Once you grasp the core of what's happening, you allow yourself to feel your way through it.

You're a visionary, and your creativity reflects that. You're able to spot a trend long before it reaches a tipping point and use that knowledge and foresight to transform any area of your life with which you're dissatisfied. The best time to tackle this process is when Jupiter transits Leo, your opposite sign, between July 16, 2014, and August 11, 2015.

During this period your business and personal partnerships expand, you have a chance to demonstrate your creative abilities, and a partner is instrumental in helping you to create a life that suits you in every way.

Pisces

You and your mutable cousins—Gemini, Virgo, and Sagittarius—are best equipped to deal with change. But for you any kind of change requires an emotional adjustment, and this is where things can get dicey.

You are in touch with your emotions, so you know when something is off kilter. But you may not know how to change whatever it is. This is when your powerful imagination comes into play. Whatever you can imagine and back with emotion can be brought into your life. Allow your creativity to explore your options. Be innovative.

For you Jupiter's transit through fellow water sign Cancer will be the best time to experiment. The dates: January 1 to July 16.

CHAPTER 11

Aspects

An aspect is the angle that planets make to other planets in a natal chart—by transit, progression, solar return, or any other system in astrology. For the purpose of this book, we primarily look at where these transiting planets hit your solar houses and the angles they make to your sun and each other. Some of these angles are beneficial, others are challenging. Think of aspects as a symbolic network of arteries and veins that transports the blood of astrology. In a natal chart these angles connect our inner and outer worlds, accentuate certain traits, and play down others. Each aspect represents a certain type of energy, so there really aren't any good or bad aspects because energy is neutral. It's what we do with the energy that counts. It comes back to free will. When transiting planets make angles to each other and to our natal planets, energy is also exchanged.

For instance, every year there is at least one very lucky day when the transiting sun and transiting Jupiter form a beneficial angle to each other—a conjunction (same sign and degree), a sextile (60 degrees apart), or a trine (120 degrees apart). In 2014 there are two such dates—July 25–26, when the sun and Jupiter are conjunct. This means that the sun's life energy and Jupiter's expansive energy combine and create, well, some magic for all of us! It's especially good for Leo and other fire signs. But since we all have Leo somewhere in our charts, these two days are lucky for the rest of us too.

If you look back to the presidential election in November 2008, Saturn in Virgo and Uranus in Pisces formed an exact opposition to each other. They were 180 degrees apart, an aspect that is like a tug-of-war. In this case the tug-of-war was between the candidate that represented the old paradigm, the established order—Saturn—and the candidate who symbolized sweeping change—Uranus.

Aspects are most powerful as they are approaching exactness. So even though a conjunction, for example, is 00 degrees of separation or a square is technically 90 degrees of separation, many astrologers use *orbs* that can be as wide as 5 or 10 degrees. Some astrologers use small orbs, but others assign larger orbs for the sun and moon and smaller orbs for other planets. The closer the orb, the more powerful the combination. If you're sensitive to transits, then, you may be feeling lucky for several days before and after July 25–26.

In terms of a natal chart, any transiting planet that is approaching an aspect with one of your natal planets is also most powerful on its approach. The traditional aspects have been used since the second century A.D. They are the conjunction, sextile, square, trine, and opposition. These aspects are considered to be the major or hard angles and are also the most power-ful. There are other minor aspects that astrologers use, but for the purpose of this chapter, we'll only talk about the traditional aspects.

Conjunction, Major Hard Aspect, 0 Degrees

This aspect is easy to identify—clusters of planets within a few degrees of each other, usually but not always in the same sign and house. But it's a complex aspect because energies combine, fuse, merge. Think of it as power and intensity, and that's true whether it's in your natal chart or is a transiting planet conjuncting your sun sign. If you have conjunctions in your natal chart, the astrologer who reads for you should address what it means and how you can use it to maximize your potential.

Sextile, Major Soft Aspect, 60 Degrees

Planets that are sextile to each other flow well to-gether, feed each other. According to house and sign, they may confer artistic ability, the gift of gab, greater imagination, higher intuition.

Square, Major Hard Aspect, 90 Degrees

Friction, angst, *oh my God, the sky is falling*: that's how squares feel in a natal chart. The sky, of course, is never falling, but the friction and angst are quite real and act as triggers for action and forward thrust. They force us to develop, evolve, and reach aggressively for our desires.

Trines, Major Soft Aspect, 120 Degrees

This aspect works like a sextile, linking energies in a harmonious way. It's associated with general ease and good fortune, and it means the same whether it's in the natal chart or by transit. People with a lot of trines in their natural charts are sometimes at a disadvantage because things come so easily to them.

Opposition, Major Hard Aspect, 180 Degrees

This aspect feels like a persistent itch that you can't reach and usually involves polarities—Taurus/Scorpio, for example, or Aries/Libra. It brings about change through conflict and sometimes represents traits we project onto others because we haven't fully integrated them into ourselves. Again the opposition applies to transits as well as to natal planets.

When checking the transits in your own chart, always keep in mind the meanings of the two planets involved, the meanings of the houses, and the meanings of the aspects.

Some other minor aspects that astrologers use are:

- the semi-square, 45 degrees. It creates irritation and friction between the planets involved.
- the septile, 51 degrees. Indicative of harmony and union in a nontraditional way. Can suggest spiritual power.
- the quincunx or inconjunct, 150 degrees separation. Indicates a need for adjustment in attitude and beliefs.

CHAPTER 12

The Astrological Neighborhood

Several years ago a Google search for the word *astrology* turned up about 40 million links. Today a Google search results in 114 million links. It suggests that as greater numbers of people search for information and insights, astrology has exploded in popularity.

You can find sites for virtually any aspect of this fascinating field, but some sites are far superior and more user friendly than others. These sites offer free natal charts, daily transits, monthly horoscopes, and political and world predictions. It's all at your fingertips. We have a blog at www.sydneyomarr.blogspot .com. In addition, here are some great astrology sites:

www.astrologyzone.com: Susan Miller's site is a favorite for neophytes and pros alike. Every month she writes about several words per sign, with detailed predictions for the month. She cites the best days for romance, finances, and career matters. She discusses new and full moons, eclipses, and their impact on your sun sign, and provides information on various aspects that are coming up in a given month. You can also obtain a free natal chart. Her site is chocked with information and is user friendly, and her predictions are eerily accurate.

www.astro.com: This site is also jammed with information. Here you can get a free natal chart, see immediately where the planets are today, use the ephemeris, and find out the geographical coordinates for a particular city. There are other interesting tidbits as well—celebrities born on a given day and fascinating and informative articles by some of the world's best astrologers. This site is perfect for the beginner, the intermediary, and the advanced astrologer.

www.moonvalleyastrologer.com: Celeste Teal is *the* expert on eclipses, a specialized area of astrology that few have researched the way she has. Her two books on eclipses are seminal works. She also provides informative articles on various aspects of astrology. If you're new to astrology, there's plenty on this site to whet your appetite. Regardless of your expertise in astrology, Celeste's site offers information for everyone.

www.astrocollege.com: Lois Rodden's site is extraordinary. This woman spent most of her life collecting birth data and then created a piece of software that is invaluable in research. For example, you can compare charts of individuals in virtually any field and discover what astrological components they have in common. Let's say you're looking for artists who all had Leo suns, Capricorn moons, and Scorpio rising. You enter those criteria, and the software delivers names. The software also provides *signatures*—a certain combination of aspects and other factors that points to particular characteristics in an individual. In addition, the site rates and sells astrology software. Lois has passed on, but her work survives.

http://astrofuturetrends.com: Author and astrologer Anthony Louis does just what the site says. He predicts future trends, covers political stuff, and provides an overall view of astrology.

www.starlightnews.com: Click on *Nancy's blog*. Here you'll find the latest predictions and insights about world affairs. Nancy's predictions about politics have been right on. Before the 2004 election she made some predictions about tight senatorial races that were totally accurate. She also called the presidential race in 2008. Since we're writing this in early 2012, we don't know yet what her predictions are for 2012, but she'll undoubtedly prove to be accurate. She receives hundreds of comments for her posts, and some of them are as informative as her posts.

www.synchrosecrets.com/synchrosecrets: About synchronicities—what they are, how they show up in our lives, what they might mean, and hundreds of stories. There are occasional posts on astrological factors—like Mercury retrogrades!

Software

In the days before computers a natal chart or anything else connected to astrology had to be configured manually, through complicated mathematical formulae that left you gasping. Astrology software has truly transformed the study of astrology and our knowledge about it. Since the late 1980s, when we began using astrology software, the choices have multiplied.

Our first piece of software was a really simply program we found at a computer store for ten bucks. It erected a chart in about sixty seconds. There it was, rising, moon, sun, planets, the houses, everything set up on the computer screen as if by magic. In the late 1990s we bought our first really terrific astrology software from Matrix for about $300. In the years since, **http://www.astrologysoftware.com** has supplied us with endless data and information and revolutionized the study of astrology.

But it's not just enough to have a great piece of software. When your computer crashes, when you receive updates that screw up, when Windows updates to a new system, you call the Matrix help line and their people walk you through it until everything works. And the employees on their help lines aren't outsourced. You won't reach India. You'll talk to someone in Michigan who is not only an astrologer, but a computer geek who knows how to fix your problem. And if by some fluke they can't fix your problem, they'll credit you for one of their other terrific programs.

The only complaint we have about Matrix is that to activate the software, you have to call or contact them through the Internet to receive a special code. If your computer crashes, if you buy a new PC or laptop . . . well, it's annoying. When you pay this much for software, you shouldn't have to obtain a special access code.

Another great piece of software is SolarFire. Astrologers are as dedicated to this program as they are to Matrix's software. Check out http://www.alabe.com for current prices. While the two programs offer similar features and capabilities, preferences seem to be individual. Both Matrix's Winstar and astrolabe's SolarFire offer many of the same features—natal charts, transits, progressed charts, solar chart, and interpretations. They both feature material about fixed stars, aspects, lunations, eclipses, and all the other important components you could possibly want or need. The main difference lies in the appearance of the charts and how the information is presented.

Kepler's astrology program—http://www.astrosoftware.com—is beautiful in its rendition of charts, interpretations, and just about anything any astrologer could use or need. We like it for its ease, its beauty. But it lacks the complexity of both Winstar and Solar-Fire. The program simply doesn't do as much.

If your exploration of astrology takes you deeper, there are other software programs that take you there. Bernadette Brady is the undisputed mistress of fixed stars. Her software program, Starlight, is remarkable not only for its accuracy, but for its presentation. You will never think of fixed stars in the same way once you play with this program. What won't make sense in a natal chart interpretation suddenly snaps into clarity when you use her software. Be sure to download a print to file version for the software—through a PDF file—so that you can maximize usage. Their website: http://www.zyntara.com.

Lois Rodden's AstroDatabank is the software that Lois Rodden developed. It contains over thirty thousand birth records, "carefully documented and coded for accuracy with the popular Rodden Rating system. AstroDatabank includes intriguing biographies, revealing personality traits, important life events, and significant relationships." For the curious, the researcher, the neophyte and pro alike.

Both Winstar and SolarFire produce computerized report software. These reports are handy for when a friend of a friend is in a fix and you don't have the time to interpret transits and progressions for the person's birth chart. Winstar also produces software on other divination systems.

Day Watch, another Winstar program, is forecasting software that is invaluable for astrologers. From their site: "Certainly it creates personalized astrological calendars, a great tool for professional astrologers and those who have an understanding of astrological terms, symbols, and technique. But Day Watch also contains a full range of onscreen and printable interpretations of events that even someone with absolutely no astrological training can read, understand, and immediately put to use in their daily lives."

At the beginning of every month we bring up our personalized calendars that tell us what is happening daily in our natal charts and also lists which planets are changing signs in that month, on what date, and which planets are turning retrograde or direct. Each month includes an ephemeris and lunar charts for the new and full moon. The program also offers various types of reports.

Keep in mind that these programs are only for Windows. They don't work with the Mac operating system. As far as we know, there's just one program for Macs—the IO Edition, developed by Time Cycles Research. It lacks the bells and whistles of Winstar, but is certainly good enough for a natal chart and transits.

Getting a Reading

So now you're ready for an astrological reading. But where do you start? Which astrologer should you use?

The best way to find an astrologer is through someone who has gotten a reading and recommends the individual. If you don't know anyone who has had an astrological reading, the next best course is to head over to the nearest bookstore and look through the astrology books. Browse through titles that interest you. Note the author's style. If the author uses a lot of astro jargon or seems to write in a depressing or heavy-handed way, move on. Once you find an author whose book you like, check to see if he or she has a Web site. Most astrologers these days have Web sites that spell out their fees, what types of readings are offered, and a contact address.

Rates for a reading vary from one astrologer to another and usually depend on what you want. Would you like just an interpretation of your natal chart? Would you like a forecast for the next six months or a year? Do you want a compatibility chart for you and your partner? Some astrologers prefer to do phone readings and record the reading. Others prefer to work through e-mail. If the astrologer you've chosen lives close to you, all the better. Have the reading done in person.

What to Expect During a Reading

Every astrological reading begins with your natal chart, so an accurate birth time is essential. It should come from your birth certificate or a parent's memory. An approximate time means the entire reading won't be as accurate. Over the years we've done way too many readings that turned out to be based on inaccurate birth times and then had to construct an accurate chart. If you don't know your time of birth, it's possible to rectify your chart based on major events in your life—the date of your marriage or divorce, a major move, the death of a parent. But this process is time consuming and rarely as accurate as an exact birth time.

A reading with an astrologer differs from a daily horoscope you find in a newspaper or even on a Web site. It's tailored to your specific chart rather than just to your sun sign. If you're getting a reading only on your birth chart, the astrologer interprets the entire chart, not just pieces of it. The astrologer looks at the signs and house placements of the various planets and the angles the planets make to each other.

If you want predictions for the next six or twelve months, the astrologer uses various techniques that are all based on your natal chart. Transits—the daily motion of the planets—have the most immediate impact on our lives, so the astrologer will first look at how the slower-moving planets—Pluto, Neptune, Uranus—impact your chart. Since they stay in the same sign for the greatest length of time, their influence can be felt for decades. The transits of both Saturn and Jupiter are taken into account too.

Usually the astrologer will pay close attention to how the transits of your chart's ruler are affecting you. If you have Scorpio rising, the transits of Pluto and Mars (the coruler) would be important. If you have Gemini rising, Mercury's transits would be important. The astrologer should also consider how eclipses and the new and full moons might affect you, particularly when there's a lunation in the same sign as your natal sun, moon, or rising.

Another predictive technique the astrologer should use is one called progression. In this technique your natal chart is progressed forward in time to the present. Since the moon is the swiftest-moving planet, moving about one progressed degree a month, the progressed chart provides timing. An astrologer can time events down to a month.

Yet another predictive technique is called the solar return chart, where your sun sign is returned to where it was at your birth. This chart's influence extends from one birthday to the next and when compared with the natal chart provides additional information and insights about what you can expect during the next twelve months.

An astrologer may also take a look at other elements in your chart, or if you have a specific question can erect an horary chart for that particular question. Horary and medical astrology are specialized fields and not all astrologers are competent to answer questions using this technique.

CHAPTER 13

By the Numbers

Even though this is an astrology book, we use numbers in some of the daily predictions because we're attempting to remain true to what Sydney Omarr did. The legendary astrologer was also a numerologist and combined the two forms in his work. So let's take a closer look at how the numbers work.

If you're familiar with numerology, you probably know your life path number, which is derived from your birth date. That number represents who you were at birth and the traits that you'll carry throughout your life. There are numerous books and Web sites that provide details on what the numbers mean regarding your life path.

But in the daily predictions, what does it mean when it's a number 9 day, and how did it get to be that number? In the dailies you'll usually find these numbers on the days when the moon is transiting from one sign to another. The system is simple: add the numbers related to the astrological sign (1 for Aries, 2 for Taurus, etc.), the year, the month, and the day.

For example, to find what number June 14, 2014, is

for a Libra, you would start with 7, the number for Libra, add 7 (the number you get when you add 2014 together), plus 6 for June, plus 5 (1+4) for the day. That would be 7+7+6+5 (sign + year + month+ day) = 25 or 7. So June 14, 2014, is a number 7 day for a Libra. It would be an 8 day for a Scorpio, the sign following Libra. So on that number 7 day Libra might be advised that his investigative and research skills are especially strong, and he should explore his spiritual beliefs and venture into the unknown.

Briefly here are the meanings of the numbers, which are included in more detail in the dailies themselves.

1) Taking the lead, getting a fresh start, a new beginning
2) Cooperation, partnership, a new relationship, sensitivity
3) Harmony, beauty, pleasures of life, warm, receptive
4) Getting organized, hard work, being methodical, rebuilding, fulfilling your obligations
5) Freedom of thought and action, change, variety, thinking outside the box
6) A service day, being diplomatic, generous, tolerant, sympathetic
7) Mystery, secrets, investigations, research, detecting deception, exploration of the unknown, of the spiritual realms
8) Your power day, financial success, unexpected money, a windfall
9) Finishing a project, looking beyond the immediate, setting your goals, reflection, expansion.

Simple, right?

Once you become accustomed to what the numbers mean for a particular day, you can adjust your attitude and thoughts accordingly. After all, how a day, week, month, or year unfolds depends more on your attitude toward yourself and your world than it does on any number or astrology sign. If you practice waking up each morning in a spirit of adventure and gratitude, pretty soon it becomes second nature, and your life shifts accordingly. Sound like magical thinking? It is. Try it, and watch your life change.

CHAPTER 14

Matters of the Heart for Taurus in 2014

To be informed is to be empowered, and astrology is a perfect tool for timing, particularly when it comes to love and romance.

In this area, we look at the transits of Venus as well as the angles Venus is making to your sun sign. If you know, for instance, when Venus is making a difficult angle to your sun sign, you can expect challenges in your love life. If you know when Venus is going to be in your sun sign, you can expect pretty smooth sailing.

There are other factors too, of course, that have a bearing on your love life. What is Mars doing at any given time? As the planet that symbolizes your sexuality, aggression, and ambition, its transits and the angles it makes to Venus and your sun sign are important. Then there are lunar transits. The moon— symbolic of your emotions, inner life, ability to nurture, and intuition—is also important. You can see how this could get complicated very quickly. So let's keep things simple and take a look at just the Venus transits in 2014. We'll pinpoint time periods for you that are both propitious and challenging for love and romance.

Venus Transits in 2014 That Make Your Heart Sing

Venus starts the year retrograde in fellow earth sign Capricorn, your solar ninth house. It turns direct, though, on January 31, and between that date and March 5 should be operating very much in your favor. If you travel during this period, love and romance may find you in unexpected, even exotic locales. Or you could meet a special someone at a seminar or workshop, in a college or graduate school class, even in a courtroom! Or you may meet someone through your career/work.

If you're in a committed relationship already, this transit boosts your commitment to each other. You and your partner may travel together to some far-flung spot in the world. It's easier to set joint goals for your relationship.

May 28–June 23: Venus is in your sign. This transit is one of the two best this year for love and romance. Your head and your heart are in the same place. Others find you appealing, like your ideas, and believe you're the one with the answers. If a romance begins during this transit, the relationship should be quite nice for you! Your muse is also up close and personal during this period. Be sure to take advantage of that by diving into your creative projects.

September 5–29: A stupendous transit! Venus moves through Virgo, your solar fifth house. While it's in this house, your love life hums along at a perfect pitch, your muse is at your beck and call, and you're having so much fun you may be tempted to just kick back and chill. Instead, use this period to find creative solutions to daily challenges, and dust off that manuscript sitting in your drawer!

During each of these transits your earth-sign qualities are enhanced and strengthened. If you're a sensual Taurus, then your sensuality is enhanced. If you're one of those Tauruses who enjoys beautiful things, then be sure you pay cash for whatever piece of art or jewelry catches your attention. Indulge yourself, but only if you can afford it.

Good Backups

July 18–August 12: Venus transits compatible water sign Cancer, your solar third house. This transit is fun for you, whether you're involved or not. Your mood is lighter, you're more social, you're eager to communicate and can strike up conversations with virtually anyone. Your intuition is more powerful too, so pay attention to your hunches.

In a romantic relationship you and your partner may be more open to communicating what you feel about each other and the relationship generally. If you're not involved when the transit starts, you could meet someone interesting in your neighborhood or through a sibling.

April 5–May 2: Venus transits compatible water sign Pisces, your solar eleventh house. This one could bring someone interesting into your life through social

163

networks or friends. Your imagination and ability to visualize what you want are quite strong during this period.

October 23–November 16: Venus transits Scorpio, your opposite sign. An intense period. Opposite attracts!

Challenging Transits

May 2–May 28: Venus transits fire sign Aries, your solar twelfth house. Unless you have a lot of fire signs in your natal chart, this won't be your favorite transit. Hidden stuff in a relationship may surface. There may be a lot of emotional drama during this period. You may be short-tempered. People around you seem to be pressing your buttons!

August 12–September 5: Venus transits fire sign Leo. This one may prompt you to strive for recognition. You may be boastful, show off, strut your stuff. These behaviors aren't innately negative, but they go against your personal grain. Or you may meet someone who exhibits these qualities.

November 16–December 10: Venus moves through fire sign Sagittarius. You may be much more independent and free-spirited during this transit.

When Love Is Practical

As an earth sign, your approach to love and romance is often practical and will be more so when Venus transits your sign, Virgo, and Capricorn. In 2014 Venus transits Capricorn twice: **January 1–31**, which we talked about at the beginning of the chapter, and from **December 10, 2014, to January 27, 2015.** During both of these transits your approach to love and romance may be more grounded and focused on goals and objectives.

Between **June 23 and July 18** Venus transits air sign Gemini. During this period your approach to love is likely to be more mental, with an emphasis on communication. For you to be seduced, a partner will have to seduce your mind first!

Another social period for you in terms of love and romance falls between **September 29 and October 23.** Venus transits Libra during this time, and you may be more interested in socializing than in spending solo time with your partner.

In the next chapter we'll take a look at what Mars is doing this year and how its transits could impact your sexuality.

CHAPTER 15

Your Sexuality and Ambition in 2014

In an earlier chapter we talked about the role of Mars in astrology. Just to reiterate, this planet rules your sexuality, physicality, ambition, and drive and can sometimes have an indirect effect on your health. In this chapter we're going to take a look at how the Mars transits in 2014 affect these areas — and, inadvertently, your love life!

Keep in mind that a positive angle between Mars and your sun sign can act as a booster rocket. A challenging angle can be frustrating. But regardless, if you're informed about how to deal with an upcoming transit, then you're empowered.

For the first two months of the year Mars is moving in direct motion in Libra, your solar sixth house of health and work. This transit could indicate that you're working diligently, perhaps as part of a team effort, and burning the candle at both ends. There could be chemistry between you and a coworker or employee. If you're self-employed, the chemistry could happen between you and a client.

It's an excellent time to network and be cooperative. In any relationship, professional or romantic, you're willing to listen to your partner's point of view. You're not as—well—stubborn as usual!

Between March 1 and May 19 Mars ceases to function at optimum levels because it moves retrograde. During this period you may revisit sexuality issues you thought were solved. or your sex life may not be as vigorous as you hoped. Also, social relationships and your team efforts may not go as planned. Something is *off*.

It's easy to feel frustrated when Mars is moving retrograde, and the best way to deal with it is to go the extra mile in everything you do. If your partner wants to see a particular movie or play that doesn't interest you, go along anyway and suggest that you have dinner at some restaurant you both enjoy. Rather than resist, try to go with the flow, whatever it is. And remember, this too shall pass! Once Mars turns direct again, you're in better shape.

Between May 19 and July 25 with Mars in direct motion again, the texture of things is similar to what it was before the retrograde began.

From July 27 to September 13 Mars transits Scorpio, your opposite sign and a sign that Mars corules. During this period it's in your solar seventh house of partnerships, and it's possible that a romantic relationship is taken to the next level. You two move in together, get engaged or married. Mars in Scorpio is a sexually charged, intense transit. You're after the absolute bottom line in everything—relationships, work, your career. You may be digging deeply and obsessively for answers in love, sex, and just about everything else.

During this transit it's important that you strike a balance between what's good for you personally and what's good for your closest partnerships.

The period from September 13 to October 26 could be somewhat stressful. Mars transits fire sign Sagittarius, your solar eighth house of shared resources. Your partner's income may come under your spotlight. You aggressively pursue additional income, may be volunteering your time on a worthy project. If you're in the midst of a divorce, the question of resources could be a bone of contention.

With Mars in Sagittarius, you may feel a powerful urge to hit the open road. Indulge yourself. Load up a backpack, grab your ATM card, and go wherever the spirit moves you.

Between October 26 and December 4 Mars transits fellow earth sign Capricorn, your solar ninth house. This period provides a window of opportunity for moving ahead professionally. Capricorn is a focused sign, so if you have a particular project you want to work on or a particular idea you want to present to bosses, clients, whoever, now is the time to do it. And fortunately Mercury turns direct the day before this transit begins, so the path of communication looks unimpeded.

While Mars is in your solar ninth house, you may not only be traveling abroad, but could be attending a workshop or seminar, taking college or grad school level classes, or could have contact with the publishing industry. So if you've got a manuscript you've written, start submitting.

From December 4, 2014, to January 12, 2015, Mars transits Aquarius, your solar tenth house—your career area. This transit certainly favors all professional matters. You may be working longer hours, but it suits you. You initiate projects and work hard to make them successful. You garner the support you need from coworkers and bosses and enter the new year with the wind at your back and a dream as your guiding light.

Other Important Dates

On November 6 there's a full moon in your sign, Mars and Pluto are in Capricorn, and Neptune is in water sign Pisces. With such an emphasis on earth signs and with Neptune in a compatible water sign, November 6 and the four days to either side of it should be quite good for you. Something reaches fruition or a culmination point—a project, a relationship, an issue.

April 15 features a lunar eclipse in Libra, with Mars in Libra forming a wide conjunction. This could bring up emotional issues related to relationships and your daily work. You may be more cooperative than you usually are!

April 29 is another important date. There's a solar eclipse in your sign, which should usher in new opportunities. Mercury is also in Taurus, suggesting that your communication skills are solid. With Mars in Libra, forming a challenging angle to the eclipse degree, you could feel stressed, but are nonetheless in a social, networking mood and use that mood to your advantage.

Another positive aspect of this eclipse is that Jupiter is in Cancer, a water sign compatible with your earth-sign sun. Jupiter expands, so the new opportunities that surface should expand your world in a significant way.

Saturn is in Scorpio, your opposite sign, until December 23. You know what this feels like since it's been there since October 2012. A Saturn opposition to your sun can be challenging, and those challenges may surface in your partnerships. You may have to assume more responsibility for a partner—romantic or business—or you may need more structure than a relationship presently provides. Once Saturn moves into Sadge, those needs and responsibilities begin to fade.

Keep a Record

In the space below, keep a brief record of how each of these transits impacts your life. Over time you may recognize patterns emerging with certain transits of Mars. With access to the Internet, you can also check on how combined transits impact your life.

Let's say that while Mars is moving through fellow earth sign Capricorn, an opportunity to travel abroad surfaces. Note the time and date, and then use the Internet to find out what the other planets were doing when this opportunity came along. You may discover that the moon was in your sign or that of another earth or water sign.

The purpose of this record is to grasp the patterns to which you're sensitive. If you don't already have a copy of your natal chart, by all means get one. Web sites that offer free natal charts are listed elsewhere in the book. The more information you have, the better prepared you'll be to take advantage of beneficial transits before they arrive!

_____

_____

_____

_____

_____

_____

_____

_____

_____

_____

_____

_____

_____

_____

_____

_____

_____

_____

_____

_____

_____

_____

_____

_____

CHAPTER 16

Career Timing for Taurus in 2014

Timing is everything, right? In terms of your career in 2014, there are some stellar dates to scrutinize closely for possible career advances and changes. With Uranus in Aries and your solar twelfth house until March 2019, your internal life will continue to offer up sudden, unexpected insights, dream guidance, and synchronicities. So pay attention to your inner self, and follow the signs!

One of the best dates for you in terms of your career and just about everything else, Taurus, occurs on April 29, with a new moon—and a solar eclipse—in your sign. Jupiter forms a wide, beneficial angle to the eclipse degree, so any new opportunities that surface are going to expand your personal life in a significant way. Mercury forms a close conjunction to the eclipse degree, and that could indicate that communication could be one of the new opportunities—writing, public speaking, a blog, Web site. Neptune forms a close, beneficial angle to this eclipse degree too. Its angle suggests higher inspiration, deeper psychic and intuitive abilities, and a spiritual slant to the new opportunities.

To prepare for this new moon, it's beneficial to make a list of what you desire, hope for, and would like to experience and achieve between this new moon in your sign and the next one in 2015. Once you make your list, backing each item with emotion, post it where you'll see it frequently—the fridge, your office. Don't obsess about it, though. Let go, and let the universe do its thing!

If you've been looking for employment, this new moon could help you find the right job at the right time. You could get a lead through a social media site, by networking with like-minded individuals, or through friends. If you've applied for college or graduate school, you could hear the news that you've been accepted around the time of this new moon.

Whenever a beneficial planet transits your career area, professional opportunities surface. This occurs between March 5 and April 5, when Venus transits Aquarius, your solar tenth house. During this period you're seeking unconventional answers and methods and have some unusual individuals on your team. Bosses and peers are receptive to your ideas, and they see you as the person with the answers. Even if a romantic attraction occurs during this period, you may be too busy to get involved. If you're involved in a relationship already, let your partner know before this transit begins that you're going to be tied up for a few weeks, getting your career in order!

During this same time period Mercury, the planet of communication, is in Pisces, a water sign that's compatible with your sun. This transit should ramp up your intuition, Taurus, so pay close attention to hunches and synchronicities. They act as guidance and confirmation. This Mercury transit stimulates your imagination too, and nothing is too far out there to consider. You of all the signs have the ability to take such ideas and make them practical.

Between April 23 and May 7 Mercury is in your sign, and you're able to express yourself extremely well and clearly. Your conscious mind is grounded, your ideas are solid, you come across as dependable. Bosses and peers are attracted to those qualities.

Venus transits your sign between May 28 and June 23, a magnificent transit when you're in synch with everything around you. During this period it seems that things go your way with barely any effort on your part. You're particularly aware of the people in your life — the roles they play, the qualities you enjoy about them, even the qualities you dislike. It's one of the most creative times for you all year. Take advantage of it in your profession.

We also like the dates between September 5 and September 29, when Venus transits fellow earth sign Virgo. This period is also one of the most creative times for you all year, with your muse up close and personal, at your beck and call 24/7. So before you commit to any particular project, test it out with your muse. Ask for a dream that clarifies your questions or that provides answers. Brainstorm with friends, family, and other creative people.

If you're unemployed then this is the ideal time to send out résumés and schedule interviews. Prospective employers will be attracted to your ideas and to you personally. You come off as smart, savvy, charming, reliable.

The other period to anticipate this year occurs

when Jupiter is transiting water sign Cancer, which is compatible with your sun. This transit is carried over from 2013 and lasts until July 16. This transit increases and expands the ways in which you communicate. You may write a novel or screenplay or a nonfiction book on a topic about which you feel passionate. You could build a Web site or start a blog that advertises your product or service or those of your company. You might even decide to go into business with a sibling, neighbor, or friend.

Just be sure that during Jupiter's transit through Cancer you focus on doing what you love. That adage applies to all areas of your life, but we're talking here specifically about your professional life. What special talents do you have? Is there some way to translate that hobby or passion into a money-making job? Look for gaps in the market that you might be able to fill. Let your entrepreneurial spirit shine. It may take you a while to come up with ideas, but once you find one that captures you, you stay with it from start to finish.

And let's not forget that Pluto is transiting fellow earth sign Capricorn and forming a strong and positive angle to your sun until 2024. This transit brings about profound changes in your professional ambitions, worldview, and educational goals. You're in the power seat.

Check out the dates in the previous chapter for Mars transits through earth signs. Those periods will be especially important professionally because Mars will be forming a beneficial angle to your sun. Your physical energy will be extraordinary, enabling you to work longer hours and take on greater responsibility.

You're able to delegate responsibility in a judicious way.

The biggest challenge with the Mars transits through fellow earth signs is learning how to balance your career with other areas of your life — your family, home, kids. This would be an ideal time to take up meditation and have some sort of regular exercise routine that keeps you fit. It might be a good idea to sign up for some yoga classes too.

You're probably wondering at this point how you're going to have time to do all this and get enough sleep every day and have fun and have down time and ... Relax, Taurus. It will all work out, somehow. There's a big faith factor involved here too: faith that you can do it all, that the universe is on your side, that you're in the right place at the right time for the right career move.

CHAPTER 17

The Big Picture for Taurus in 2014

Welcome to 2014, Taurus! It's a 9 year for you, with many beginnings and endings. It's your year to tie up loose ends; an old cycle is ending and a new cycle is about to begin. You're making room in your life for new relationships, a new job, perhaps even a new career path. Now that the tumult of 2012 and the realignment of 2013 are behind you, you're ready for everything the universe brings your way.

So let's look at how specific areas of your life may be impacted and which dates will be of vital importance to you.

Romance/Creativity

One of the most romantic and creative times for you all year occurs between May 28 and June 23, when Venus transits your sign. During this period your muse is at your beck and call, and you feel so creative that everything you touch illustrates how your muse is working for you. You feel more self-confident. Others pick up on that vibe and are attracted to you, your ideas, your persona, your creative projects. So if you have creative products ready, start submitting and exhibiting them, doing whatever you need to do in order to advertise your work.

If a relationship begins during this period, it's likely to be sensuous and deeply satisfying for you. The romantic interests you attract are a reflection of who you are within the deepest parts of your soul. If you're already involved in a relationship, this transit helps to define it. You and your partner may deepen your commitment to each other

The other terrific period for romance and creativity occurs between September 5 and 29, when Venus transits fellow earth sign Virgo, your solar fifth house. This transit stimulates you to do whatever it is you most enjoy. If it's travel, you go traveling. If your passion is politics, you dive into the political arena in some way. It's a perfect time for romance, the kind of romance that entails candlelit dinners, midnight walks on a beach, kayaking through some mysterious shaded part of a river . . . you get the idea.

Between January 1 and July 16 Jupiter is completing its transit of Cancer that began last year. Cancer is a water sign compatible with your earth-sign sun, Taurus, so this transit should be expanding all your communication venues. Your communication skills are heightened during this period, and this makes it easier for you to talk about what you feel in any relationship.

Jupiter's transit through Cancer forms a strong angle to your sun and heightens your intuition, nurturing qualities, and love of home and family (that's the Cancer part of it!). If you're in a committed relationship already, you and your partner may decide to move in together or get married.

On July 16 Jupiter enters Leo, where it will be until August 11, 2015. If you have a lot of fire-sign planets in your natal chart, this transit will benefit you tremendously. If not, it could create excesses in some area of your life, but you still benefit. Jupiter turns retrograde on December 8 and doesn't turn direct again until April 8, 2015.

Other excellent dates:

January 15, when a full moon in Cancer shines brightly with Jupiter.

July 18–August 12, when Venus joins Jupiter in Cancer. This period infuses your love life with harmony and brings your muse up close and personal.

Be sure to consult the chapter Matters of the Heart for more details on good dates for romance and creative ventures.

Career

Jupiter's transit through Cancer, of course, will help every facet of your life, even your career. The caveat with career matters, though, is that if you're doing something you love, you benefit tremendously. If you're working in a field that doesn't excite you, that has become rather humdrum and routine, Jupiter, Mars, and your ruler, Venus, could help you to break away and find something that is more aligned with your passions.

Let's take a closer look at the beneficial career times:

January 11–31: Mercury transits your career area, making this period an excellent one for communication with bosses and peers. Pitch your ideas, gather your support among coworkers. Think as far outside the box as you dare, then allow your practical Taurus sun to translate these abstract concepts, to ground them. During this period peers and bosses are impressed with your work, skills, and organizational talents. A promotion or raise could be forthcoming.

March 5–April 5: During this period while Venus transits your career area your professional life hums along at a perfect pitch. This is the time to implement new projects, especially those that have captured your passions.

The new moon in your career area occurs on January 30 and should usher in new professional opportunities. Uranus forms a tight, beneficial angle to this new moon, suggesting that opportunities seem to come out of the blue. Just be ready to seize them.

Between December 4, 2014, and January 13, 2015, Mars transits Aquarius, your solar tenth house. This period will be highly energetic and active, and you'll feel you can do it all. Guard against spreading yourself too thinly. It's a great time to brainstorm with coworkers.

Finances

Let's look at Venus transits first for beneficial dates for finances. Your solar second house, which rules money, is in Gemini. The period to watch for, then, falls between June 23 and July 18. During this three-week period, you could get a raise, bonus, unexpected insurance, or royalty check, or someone could repay money they owe you. You may feel an urge to spend on a luxury item—jewelry, for instance, or art.

Once Jupiter enters Leo on July 16, you could see some spikes in expenses related to your home. Jupiter's transit through Leo lasts until late June 2015. It could result in an expansion in your home—you move, add a room, buy property, all of which would cost money. But not to worry, Taurus. You have the money to spend.

May 28 features a new moon in Gemini and your financial area. New opportunities surface in finances, and with Uranus forming a wide, harmonious angle, the new opportunities may surface unexpectedly.

Mercury Retrogrades

Every year Mercury—the planet of communication and travel—turns retrograde three times. During these periods it's wise not to sign contracts (unless you don't mind renegotiating when Mercury is moving direct), to check and recheck travel plans, and to communicate as succinctly as possible. Refrain from buying any large-ticket items or electronics during this time too. Often computers and appliances go on the fritz, cars act up, data is lost . . . you get the idea. Be sure to back up all files before the dates below:

February 6–28: Mercury retrograde in Pisces, your solar eleventh house. This one impacts your friendships and social circles. Mercury slips back into Aquarius before it turns direct, so it impacts your career too.

June 7–July 1: Mercury retrograde in Cancer, your solar third house. This retrograde affects communication and travel. Be sure to make travel plans on either side of the retrograde period. If you have to travel while Mercury is retrograde, regard it as an adventure!

October 4–25: Mercury retrograde in Scorpio, your solar seventh house. This one impacts your business and romantic partnerships. You and a partner may rehash old issues. There are likely to be communication mix-ups and general confusion about priorities.

Eclipses

Solar eclipses tend to trigger external events that bring about change according to the sign and house in which they fall. Lunar eclipses trigger inner, emotional events according to the sign and house in which they fall. Any eclipse marks both beginnings and endings. The solar and lunar eclipse in a pair falls in opposite signs. If you're interested in detailed information on eclipses, take a look at Celeste Teal's excellent and definitive book, *Eclipses: Predicting World Events & Personal Transformation.*

If you were born under or around the time of an eclipse, it's to your advantage to take a look at your birth chart to find out exactly where the eclipses will impact you.

Most years feature four eclipses—two solar, two

lunar—with the set separated by about two weeks. Let's take a closer look.

April 15: Lunar eclipse in Libra, your solar sixth house. This may bring up emotional issues related to your daily work routine or health. It should be a positive eclipse, though, so go with the flow and enjoy!

April 29: Solar eclipse in your sign. This eclipse should bring plenty of new opportunities that are personally satisfying. You may have to give up something before you can take advantage of these opportunities, but it won't be a difficult choice to make! With Mercury forming a close conjunction to the eclipse degree and Jupiter forming a beneficial angle to it, be on your toes and ready to seize the opportunity as soon as it occurs.

October 8: Lunar eclipse in Aries, your solar twelfth house. Uranus is closely conjunct the moon, so you can expect sudden and unexpected emotional reactions to something that surfaces from your own unconscious. It could be a past-life memory or something from early childhood, and its appearance catches you off guard.

October 23: Solar eclipse in Scorpio, your solar seventh house. New partnership opportunities. If you're already in a committed relationship, this eclipse could deepen your commitment—you get engaged or married. You also could find exactly the right partner for your business. This eclipse is at 0 degrees Scorpio and so is Venus, so it's apt to be quite positive for you.

The Luckiest Days of 2014

Every year there are one or two days when Jupiter and the sun meet up, and luck, serendipity, and expansion are the hallmarks. This year those days fall on July 25–26. Circle the dates. Do whatever you enjoy!

CHAPTER 18

Eighteen Months of Day-by-Day Predictions: July 2013 to December 2014

Moon sign times are calculated for Eastern Standard Time and Eastern Daylight Time. Please adjust for your local time zone.

JULY 2013

Monday, July 1 (Moon into Taurus, 4:44 p.m.) It's another mystery day. Look behind closed doors. Secrets, intrigue, confidential information play a role. You might feel best working on your own. It's best to hold off on making any final decisions for a couple of days.

Tuesday, July 2 (Moon in Taurus) With the moon in your first house today, you're particularly sensitive to others' feelings now. You could be somewhat moody, shifting from happy one moment, sad the next, then back again. You're dealing with your self-awareness, appearance, and the person you are becoming. It's all about your health and your emotional self: how you feel and how you feel about yourself.

Wednesday, July 3 (Moon in Taurus)　　The moon is on your ascendant today, and so you're fired up, Taurus, recharged for the month ahead. Your face is in front of the public. Post your good news on Facebook. Your appearance and personality shine. Your feelings and thoughts are aligned.

Thursday, July 4 (Moon into Gemini, 4:23 a.m.) It's a number 1 day, so you're at the top of your cycle. It's a great time for initiating new projects, launching new ideas, or brainstorming for new ways of making money. You take the lead on something new as you get a fresh start. Follow your heart. Happy Independence Day!

Friday, July 5 (Moon in Gemini)　　The moon is in your second house today. Money and material goods are important to you now and give you a sense of security, Taurus. You may be dealing with payments and collecting what's owed to you. Look at your priorities in handling your income. Expect emotional experiences related to money.

Saturday, July 6 (Moon into Cancer, 5:14 p.m.) You come out of your shell now. You communicate well. You're warm and receptive to what others say. Spread your good news. Ease up on routines. Your charm and wit are appreciated. Play your hunches.

Sunday, July 7 (Moon in Cancer)　　Saturn turns direct in your seventh house today. You tend to have very strict ideas about partnerships and marriage and a restrained attitude about sex. You could face some difficulties related to a contract. It's best to keep close tabs on someone who might try to manipulate you. It's difficult to go with the flow.

Monday, July 8 (Moon in Cancer)   There's a new moon in your third house today. That means there are new opportunities, particularly related to any community work. It's a great day to let others know your thoughts, but avoid getting overly emotional. That's especially true when dealing with siblings, other relatives, or neighbors.

Tuesday, July 9 (Moon into Leo, 5:48 a.m.)   It's a number 6 day. A domestic adjustment works out for the best. You could face emotional outbursts or someone making unfair demands. Be understanding, and avoid confrontations. Offer advice and support, but do it in a diplomatic way.

Wednesday, July 10 (Moon in Leo)   With the moon in your fourth house, you feel a close tie to your roots today. A parent could play an important role. You're dealing with the foundations of who you are and who you are becoming. It's a good day for dream recall. Retreat to a private place for meditation.

Thursday, July 11 (Moon into Virgo, 5:12 p.m.) Business discussions go well. You could pull off a financial coup. It's your power day, your day to play it your way. Unexpected money arrives. It's a great day for buying a lottery ticket. Financial gain is at hand.

Friday, July 12 (Moon in Virgo)   The moon is in
your fifth house today. You feel a sudden surge of inspiration, a creative urge that helps you break through
a block. In romance there's more depth and understanding in a relationship. Children play an important
role in your day. So do pets!

Saturday, July 13 (Moon in Virgo)   Mars goes direct in your third house today. That means there's a
release of energy for educational goals. It's also an
excellent time to pursue an interest in community
work. Try not to get overly aggressive with siblings. If
you're a writer, it's a good time to submit a manuscript.

Sunday, July 14 (Moon into Libra, 2:41 a.m.)   It's
a number 2 day. Use your intuition to get a sense of
your day. Be kind and understanding. Cooperation,
especially with partners, is highlighted. Don't make
waves. Don't rush or show resentment; let things develop. Marriage plays a key role.

Monday, July 15 (Moon in Libra)   With the
moon in your sixth house today, the emphasis turns to
your daily work and health. Help others, especially if
you can serve as a mediator in a dispute. Be careful
not to overlook any seemingly minor matters that
could take on importance. Keep up with your exercise
plan, and watch your diet.

Tuesday, July 16 (Moon into Scorpio, 9:25 a.m.)
Persevere to get things done today. Don't get sloppy.
Take care of your obligations. You're building founda-

tions for an outlet for your creativity. Emphasize quality.

Wednesday, July 17 (Moon in Scorpio)   Uranus goes retrograde in your twelfth house today and stays that way until December 17. That means you might be doing some soul-searching about matters from the deep past. You could be getting flashes of inspiration. Matters are somewhat unpredictable over the next few months. Avoid going to extremes. Pushing yourself too hard could result in accidents. Watch your step! Be careful about talking on your cell and driving.

Thursday, July 18 (Moon into Sagittarius, 12:55 p.m.)   It's a number 6 day. Service to others is the theme of the day. You offer advice and support. Diplomacy wins the way. A domestic adjustment works out for the best. Be understanding, and avoid confrontations.

Friday, July 19 (Moon in Sagittarius)   The moon is in your eighth house today. Your experiences are more intense than usual. You have a strong sense of duty and feel obligated to fulfill your promises. If you are planning on making a major purchase, make sure that you and your partner are in agreement. Otherwise you could encounter intense emotional resistance. You could be dealing with a mystery of the unknown, such as what happens after death.

Saturday, July 20 (Moon into Capricorn, 1:40 p.m.) Mercury goes direct in your third house today. Any confusion, miscommunication, and delays, especially related to siblings and other family members, recede into the past. Things move more smoothly now. You get your message across without getting overly emotional, and everything works better, including computers and other electronic equipment.

Sunday, July 21 (Moon in Capricorn)   The moon is in your ninth house today. You're a dreamer and a thinker. You may feel a need to get away now, a break from the usual routine. Pursue a new idea. Are you ready to plan a long trip?

Monday, July 22 (Moon into Aquarius, 1:08 p.m.) Venus moves into your fifth house today. You feel a strong attraction to the opposite sex. You're popular and well liked. You also get along well with children and young people. Any creative talent in the arts is highlighted. There's also a full moon in your tenth house, indicating that you gain insight into a matter related to your profession or career.

Tuesday, July 23 (Moon in Aquarius)   You gain an elevation in prestige related to your profession and career. Business is highlighted. Material success and financial security play a role in your day. You make a strong emotional commitment now to your profession or a role in public life.

Wednesday, July 24 (Moon into Pisces, 1:23 p.m.) Enjoy the harmony, beauty, and pleasures of life. Beautify your home. Your imagination is keen now. You're curious and inventive. You communicate well.

You're warm and receptive to what others say. Your attitude determines everything today.

Thursday, July 25 (Moon in Pisces)   The moon is in your eleventh house today. You join a group of friends or like-minded individuals in pursuit of a common goal. You help the group, and you gain from the group energy. Follow your wishes and dreams, and make sure that they are still an expression of who you are. Social consciousness plays a role.

Friday, July 26 (Moon into Aries, 4:30 p.m.)   It's a number 5 day. Variety is the spice of life. Think outside the box. Take risks, experiment. Release old structures; get a new point of view. You're versatile, changeable. However, be careful not to spread out and diversify too much.

Saturday, July 27 (Moon in Aries)   The new moon is in your twelfth house today. You tend to look inward now, and by doing so subconscious motivations surface and point you toward new ideas, new possibilities. Best to work behind the scenes, away from the confusion and emotional turmoil. Your absence may create a doorway to a new opportunity.

Sunday, July 28 (Moon into Taurus, 11:44 p.m.)   It's your mystery day, Taurus. Like yesterday, it's best to keep your own counsel today as you delve deep into a matter. Look behind closed doors for answers. Knowledge is essential to success. Gather information, but don't make any absolute decisions until tomorrow.

Monday, July 29 (Moon in Taurus)   The moon is in your first house today. You're dealing with the person you are becoming. You're sensitive to other people's feelings now. It's all about your health and emotional self. Your feelings and thoughts are aligned.

Tuesday, July 30 (Moon in Taurus)   The moon is on your ascendant today. That means you get recharged for the month ahead. Your face is in the public. The way you see yourself now is the way others see you, what you show the public of yourself. You're physically vital, and relations with the opposite sex go well.

Wednesday, July 31 (Moon into Gemini, 10:42 a.m.) It's a number 1 day. You're at the top of your cycle today. Get out and meet new people, have new experiences, do something you've never done before. Explore and discover. Your creativity is highlighted. Originality is stressed. Refuse to deal with people who have closed minds.

AUGUST 2013

Thursday, August 1 (Moon in Gemini)   The moon is in your second house today. So it's a good day for dealing with money issues. Pay what you owe, and collect what others owe you. You tend to equate your financial assets with emotional security now. Look at your priorities in handling your income.

Friday, August 2 (Moon into Cancer, 11:30 p.m.) It's a number 8 day, your power day and your day to play it your way. It's a good day to buy a lotto ticket; take a chance. Look for a windfall. Business dealings go well.

Saturday, August 3 (Moon in Cancer)   The moon is in your third house today. You can be quite opinionated, especially when talking with siblings, other family members, or neighbors. Try to stay in control of your emotions. You tend to be affected by matters from the past. Best to let it go. Expect some short trips as you take care of business.

Sunday, August 4 (Moon in Cancer)   Your home and personal environment are especially important for you today. Your intuition is highlighted, and so is your sensitivity. Keep your opinions to yourself. Don't allow other people's moods to bring you down. Tend to loved ones; do something with your children or sweetheart.

Monday, August 5 (Moon into Leo, 11:58 a.m.) It's a number 3 day. That means it's a good day to relax, enjoy yourself, recharge your batteries. Have fun today in preparation for tomorrow's discipline and focus. You can influence people now with your upbeat attitude. In romance you're an ardent and loyal lover.

Tuesday, August 6 (Moon in Leo)   With the new moon in your fourth house today, opportunities related to your home come your way. If you're selling your house, you have a good chance of getting a strong offer now. It's a good day for developing or working on a home-based business. With Uranus trine to the moon, you could be in for some pleasant surprises.

Wednesday, August 7 (Moon into Virgo, 10:58 p.m.)
It's a number 5 day. That means it's a good day to promote new ideas. You're versatile, changeable. Be careful not to spread out and diversify too much. Freedom of thought and action is key. A change of scenery would work to your advantage.

Thursday, August 8 (Moon in Virgo)   Mercury moves into your fourth house today. That means there's a lot of discussions taking place in the home. You communicate well with family members and get your ideas across. There could be some changes going on in your home. You have a hard time relaxing there now.

Friday, August 9 (Moon in Virgo)   The moon is in your fifth house today. You're emotionally in touch with your creative side now. You're feeling joyous and creative. Sex for pleasure is highlighted. You feel strongly attached to loved ones and protective of children. Be aware that your emotions tend to overpower your intellect.

Saturday, August 10 (Moon into Libra, 8:09 a.m.)
It's a number 8 day, your power day and your day to play it your way. Think big and act big! Unexpected money arrives. You have a chance to expand, to gain recognition, even fame and power.

Sunday, August 11 (Moon in Libra)   With the moon in your sixth house today, the emphasis turns to your daily work and service to others. Attend to all the details, Taurus. Be careful not to overlook any seemingly minor matters that could take on importance. Keep up with your exercise plan, and watch your diet.

Monday, August 12 (Moon into Scorpio, 3:19 p.m.)
It's a number 1 day, and you're at the top of your cycle. You're inventive and make connections that others overlook. You're determined and courageous today. You can take the lead now and get a fresh start, a new beginning. Don't be afraid to turn in a new direction. Trust your hunches; intuition is highlighted.

Tuesday, August 13 (Moon in Scorpio)   The moon is in your seventh house today. You communicate well with a spouse or partner. It's all about working together. A contract or lawsuit could play a role. You get along well with others now, but it's a challenge to remain detached and objective.

Wednesday, August 14 (Moon into Sagittarius, 8:05 p.m.)   You're innovative and creative and communicate well. You're well grounded, Taurus, and keep everyone in balance today. Your artistic talents are highlighted. Enjoy the harmony, beauty, and pleasures of life.

Thursday, August 15 (Moon in Sagittarius)   The moon is in your eighth house today. You pursue a mystical matter. It could involve life after death or past lives, even hauntings or ghost hunting. You dig deep for information. You could become part of a group or movement dedicated to raising people's awareness.

Friday, August 16 (Moon into Capricorn, 10:26 p.m.)
Venus moves into your sixth house today. You enjoy your work now and get along with fellow workers. The work environment is harmonious and could be conducive to an office romance. If you were worn out yesterday, you're feeling much better.

Saturday, August 17 (Moon in Capricorn) The moon is in your ninth house today. You're feeling as if you need to break out of your usual routine, or it could turn into a rut, Taurus. Travel or higher education plays a role. Plan a trip or sign up for a seminar or workshop. A foreign country or person of foreign birth could play a role.

Sunday, August 18 (Moon into Aquarius, 11:07 p.m.)
It's a number 7 day, a mystery day. You keep an eye on what's going on around you. You quickly come to a conclusion and wonder why others don't see what you see. You work best on your own today. Make sure that you see things as they are, not as you wish them to be. Knowledge is essential to success.

Monday, August 19 (Moon in Aquarius) The moon is in your tenth house today. Professional concerns take on more importance. You could get a promotion, raise, or pat on the back. You're more responsive to the needs and moods of a group and the public in general. You move up the ladder.

Tuesday, August 20 (Moon into Pisces, 11:44 p.m.)
There's a full moon in your tenth house today. You gain a big boost in prestige now related to your profession. You harvest what you've sown. Business dealings go well. Your life is more public than usual. You're more emotional and warm toward coworkers.

Wednesday, August 21 (Moon in Pisces) The moon is in your eleventh house today. You have deeper contact with friends now. You find strength in numbers and meaning through associates and groups. You work for the common good. Capricorn and Virgo play a role in your day.

Thursday, August 22 (Moon in Pisces) Imagination is highlighted. Watch for psychic events, synchronicities. Keep track of your dreams, including your daydreams. Ideas are ripe. You can tap deeply into the collective unconscious for inspiration. Universal knowledge, eternal truths, deep spirituality are the themes of the day.

Friday, August 23 (Moon into Aries, 2:13 a.m.)
It's a number 3 day. Your attitude determines everything today. Spread your good news. You're innovative and creative and communicate well. Enjoy the harmony, beauty, and pleasures of life. Beautify your home now, Taurus.

Saturday, August 24 (Moon in Aries) The moon is in your twelfth house today. You might feel a need to withdraw and work on your own. Watch what you say now and think carefully before you act. There's a tendency to undo all the positive actions you've taken. Avoid any self-destructive behavior. Be aware of hidden enemies.

Sunday, August 25 (Moon into Taurus, 8:14 a.m.)
It's another 5 day, and that means change and variety are highlighted. For example, a change of scenery would work to your advantage. You're seeking new horizons now. Approach the day with an unconventional mindset. Think freedom, no restrictions. Think outside the box. Take risks, experiment.

Monday, August 26 (Moon in Taurus)   With the moon on your ascendant, your appearance and personality shine today. You're recharged for the remainder of the month, and this makes you more appealing to the public. You're physically vital, and relations with the opposite sex go well.

Tuesday, August 27 (Moon into Gemini, 6:08 p.m.)
Mars moves into your fourth house and stays there until October 15. You're physically vital, and it's a good time for do-it-yourself repair work on your home. There's strong energy in your home environment. You have an aggressive drive for security. There's also a tendency now to get into arguments with family members.

Wednesday, August 28 (Moon in Gemini)   The moon is in your second house today. You tend to react emotionally to an event in your life related to money or your values. You identify emotionally with your possessions or whatever you value. Look at your priorities in handling your income. Watch your spending.

Thursday, August 29 (Moon in Gemini) Your mind moves quickly from one thought to another. A change of scenery works to your benefit. It's a good day to take a short trip to visit relatives or friends. Get out and have some fun today. It's also a good day to express yourself in writing.

Friday, August 30 (Moon into Cancer, 6:33 a.m.) It's a number 1 day. You're inventive and make connections that others overlook. You're determined and courageous today. Trust your hunches; intuition is highlighted. You get a fresh start. In romance something new is developing.

Saturday, August 31 (Moon in Cancer) Your mental abilities are strong now, and you have an emotional need to express your ideas. You write from a deep place today. It's a good day for journaling. Your thinking may be unduly influenced by things from the past. Female relatives play a role now.

SEPTEMBER 2013

Sunday, September 1 (Moon into Leo, 7:02 p.m.) Finish whatever you've been working on, and make room for something new. But don't start anything today. Visualize the future; set your goals, then make them so. Strive for universal appeal.

Monday, September 2 (Moon in Leo)   The moon is in your fourth house today. You feel close to your roots now. Spend time with your family and other loved ones. Stick close to home, if possible. A parent plays a role. It's a good day to work on a home-repair project.

Tuesday, September 3 (Moon in Leo)   Romance feels majestic, and you want the world to know and see. Dress boldly. You're creative and passionate today, impulsive and honest. It's a good day to take a gamble.

Wednesday, September 4 (Moon into Virgo, 5:45 a.m.) It's a number 3 day. Your attitude determines everything, Taurus. You communicate well now. You're curious and inventive. Your imagination is keen; ideas bubble forth. Your popularity is on the rise.

Thursday, September 5 (Moon in Virgo)   There's a new moon in your fifth house today. New opportunities come your way related to a creative project. You get a fresh start, a new beginning. With Jupiter forming a sextile with Virgo, those opportunities are enhanced. You can take the initiative now and expand upon whatever you are doing.

Friday, September 6 (Moon into Libra, 2:14 p.m.) You're seeking new horizons today. Think outside the box. Take risks, experiment. Get ready for changes. Release old structures; get a new point of view. You're versatile, changeable. Be careful not to spread out and diversify too much.

Saturday, September 7 (Moon in Libra) The moon is in your sixth house today. It's another service day. Others rely on you for help. So what else is new, Taurus! Help them, but don't deny your own needs. Visit someone who is ill; do a good deed. Pay attention to any health matters now. Exercise, and watch your diet.

Sunday, September 8 (Moon into Scorpio, 8:45 p.m.) It's your mystery day, Taurus. You venture into the unknown. Secrets, intrigue, confidential information play a role in your day. Gather information, but don't make any absolute decisions until tomorrow. Go with the flow. Maintain your emotional balance.

Monday, September 9 (Moon in Scorpio) Mercury moves into your sixth house today. You do well in any work that involves mental or physical focus. You could be fixating on the details. You also might be thinking too much about your health or diet now or about how you can help someone in need.

Tuesday, September 10 (Moon in Scorpio) The moon is in your seventh house today. The focus turns to partnerships now, both personal and professional. Be careful how you deal with disagreements. Any conflict will be more emotional than usual. It's difficult to remain detached and objective.

Wednesday, September 11 (Moon into Sagittarius, 1:36 a.m.) Venus moves into your seventh house today and stays there until October 7. It's a great time for romantic and business partnerships. Things will be going so well in the coming weeks that you might just want to sit back and relax. That, however, could be a mistake. Take advantage of this time. You can get a contract now.

Thursday, September 12 (Moon in Sagittarius) The moon is in your eighth house today. Take care of any matters related to taxes, insurance, or investments. Be aware that emotions can get intense now, especially when dealing with shared resources. Metaphysics could play a role in your day. You could be dealing with a mystery of the unknown, such as what happens after death.

Friday, September 13 (Moon into Capricorn, 4:56 a.m.) It's a number 3 day. Your charm and wit are appreciated today. Your imagination is working overtime; you're curious and inventive. You communicate well, and you're warm and receptive to what others say.

Saturday, September 14 (Moon in Capricorn) The moon is in your ninth house today. You're a dreamer and a thinker. You yearn for a new experience. You may feel a need to get away now, a break from the usual routine. Foreigners or a foreign country plays a role in your day.

Sunday, September 15 (Moon into Aquarius, 7:06 a.m.) Change and variety are highlighted now. Think freedom, no restrictions. Release old structures; get a new point of view. It's a good day to take a risk, experiment. Promote new ideas. Find a new outlook that fits current circumstances and what you know.

Monday, September 16 (Moon in Aquarius)   The moon is in your tenth house today. Professional concerns are the focus of the day. Business is highlighted. You're surging ahead, seeking or achieving a boost in prestige, an advancement, an award, a raise. Your life is more public. You're more emotional and warm toward coworkers, but avoid blurring the boundary between your professional and personal lives.

Tuesday, September 17 (Moon into Pisces, 8:59 a.m.) Look beneath the surface for the reasons others are shifting their points of view. Dig deep for information, but don't make any final decisions on what you uncover until tomorrow. Keep any secrets entrusted to you. Avoid confusion and conflicts.

Wednesday, September 18 (Moon in Pisces)   The moon is in your eleventh house today. Friends play an important role in your day, especially Capricorn and Virgo. You get together with a group of like-minded individuals and work toward a common goal. Focus on your wishes and dreams, and make sure that they are still a reflection of who you are.

Thursday, September 19 (Moon into Aries, 11:58 a.m.)   There's a full moon in your eleventh house today. You can reap what you've sown now with your involvement in a group or organization. Your wishes and dreams are realized. Think abundance. You have a chance to expand. Friends play an important role.

Friday, September 20 (Moon in Aries)   Pluto goes direct in your ninth house today, where it will remain until 2024. That releases more energy for long-distance travel and higher education. You're moving forward and outward. Keep in mind that Pluto transforms everything that is not needed.

Saturday, September 21 (Moon into Taurus, 5:34 p.m.) Partnerships play an important role in your day. Cooperation is highlighted. Use your intuition to get a sense of your day. Be kind and understanding, especially with someone who is nagging. Don't make waves. Don't rush or show resentment; let things develop.

Sunday, September 22 (Moon in Taurus)   The moon is in your first house today. You're feeling somewhat sensitive to other people's feelings. You may feel moody—withdrawn one moment, happy the next, then sad. It's all about your emotional self. Your thoughts and feelings are aligned.

Monday, September 23 (Moon in Taurus)   It's a good day to cultivate new ideas, but make sure that they're down-to-earth. You're feeling recharged, and that makes you more appealing to the public. You're physically vital, and relations with the opposite sex go well. Health and physical activity are highlighted.

Tuesday, September 24 (Moon into Gemini, 2:35 a.m.)   Variety is the spice of life. Think freedom, no restrictions. Change and variety are highlighted now. Approach the day with an unconventional mindset. Release old structures; get a new point of view.

Wednesday, September 25 (Moon in Gemini) The moon is in your second house today. Money and material goods are important to you now and give you a sense of security. You may be dealing with payments and collecting what's owed to you. Look at your priorities in handling your income. Expect emotional experiences related to money.

Thursday, September 26 (Moon into Cancer, 2:25 p.m.) You work best on your own today. Secrets, intrigue, confidential information play a role. Knowledge is essential to success. Express your desires, but avoid self-deception. Maintain your emotional balance.

Friday, September 27 (Moon in Cancer) The moon is in your third house today. It's a good day for expressing yourself through writing. Take what you know, and share it with others. As you go about your everyday life, look to the big picture. Expect an invitation to a social event.

Saturday, September 28 (Moon in Cancer) You could feel moody today and overly sensitive. It might seem as if the world is out to get you. It's not. Take plenty of breaks from whatever you're doing. That will help you clear your head and improve your focus when you return to work. Water plays a prominent role; you feel a need to be near it.

Sunday, September 29 (Moon into Leo, 2:58 a.m.) Mercury moves into your seventh house today. You communicate well in public, especially when you're dealing with bright and articulate people. It's a good day for you to mediate a dispute or counsel someone in need of help.

Monday, September 30 (Moon in Leo)   The moon is in your fourth house today. You're dealing with the foundations of who you are, Taurus, and who you are becoming. Retreat to a private place for meditation. It's a good day for dream recall. It's best to work on your own and stay focused. It's a good time to eliminate a bad habit.

OCTOBER 2013

Tuesday, October 1 (Moon into Virgo, 1:53 p.m.) You start the month at the top of your cycle, Taurus. It's a great day to cultivate new ideas, especially if they're down-to-earth. Stress originality. Trust your hunches; intuition is highlighted. Explore, discover, and create.

Wednesday, October 2 (Moon in Virgo)   With the moon in your fifth house today, you're emotionally in touch with your creative side. There's also greater depth in a love relationship and more involvement with any children or pets in your life. Make sure that you're not overly protective of children. They need room to grow.

Thursday, October 3 (Moon into Libra, 10:00 p.m.) Have some fun today in preparation for tomorrow's discipline and focus. Make time to listen to others. Your charm and wit are appreciated. Spread your good news; you communicate well.

Friday, October 4 (Moon in Libra)   New opportunities come your way, and you need to act today! Pay attention to details. You can uncover something significant related to your daily work. A matter related to your health becomes much clearer now.

Saturday, October 5 (Moon in Libra)   Relationship issues figure prominently in your day. This is a great day to schedule an adventurous encounter with your significant other. Your friend is apt to be feeling as excited and enthusiastic about the day as you are. It's also a day for feeding your creative juices. You might visit a museum or art gallery opening.

Sunday, October 6 (Moon into Scorpio, 3:33 a.m.) You get along well with others now. You can fit in just about anywhere. Loved ones and partners are more important than usual. A legal matter comes to your attention. You comprehend the nuances of a situation, but it's difficult to go with the flow.

Monday, October 7 (Moon in Scorpio)   Venus moves into your eighth house today. Your emotions are running strong now. You might be feeling somewhat possessive or jealous. Joint finances play a role. You could gain personally through a partner's inheritance. Money and success seem to come easily. In romance you're an ardent and loyal lover. But try to avoid any jealousy or possessiveness.

Tuesday, October 8 (Moon into Sagittarius, 7:22 a.m.) It's a number 8 day, and you're in the power seat. You're ambitious and goal-oriented. You attract financial success. You're confident, and material gain is within reach, if not already here. Be aware that you're playing with power, so try not to hurt anyone.

Wednesday, October 9 (Moon in Sagittarius) The moon is in your eighth house today. You could be feeling vulnerable now about your partner's income. Issues about taxes, a mortgage, or insurance arise. It's an excellent time to have a living will drawn up. It's also a great time to explore the real mysteries, i.e., life after death, past lives, and future lives.

Thursday, October 10 (Moon into Capricorn, 10:18 a.m.) You're at the top of your cycle again. You get a fresh start, a new beginning. You're determined and courageous today. Stress originality. You attract creative people to your side. In romance something new is developing.

Friday, October 11 (Moon in Capricorn) The moon is in your ninth house today. You're a dreamer and a thinker. You're captivated by new ideas and philosophies. You may feel a need to get away now, a break from the usual routine. You're feeling restless and yearn for a new experience.

Saturday, October 12 (Moon into Aquarius, 1:00 p.m.) You're innovative and creative and communicate well today. But make time to listen to others. Your charm and wit are appreciated. Spread your good news. If you allow yourself free time, to fill in whatever creative way you desire, then your spirits will soar, as will your productivity.

Sunday, October 13 (Moon in Aquarius) Groups and social events are highlighted now. Your individuality is stressed, and your visionary abilities are heightened. You get a new perspective. Play your hunches. Look beyond the immediate. Look to your wishes and dreams.

Monday, October 14 (Moon into Pisces, 4:06 p.m.) It's a number 5 day. That means change and variety are highlighted now. Think freedom; think outside the box. No restrictions. Your creativity, personal grace, and magnetism are highlighted.

Tuesday, October 15 (Moon in Pisces) Mars moves into your fifth house today, Taurus. You put out a lot of energy toward the pleasures of life now. You have an active and aggressive sex drive. You can also apply the Mars energy toward expanding your creative base. You love to compete, but avoid any petty jealousies or acting like a bad loser.

Wednesday, October 16 (Moon into Aries, 8:19 p.m.) It's a number 7 day, your mystery day, Taurus. Look beneath the surface for the reasons others are shifting their points of view, "changing their tune." Maintain your emotional balance. Your challenge today is to be independent without feeling isolated. You detect deception and recognize insincerity with ease. But don't make any final decisions on what you uncover until tomorrow.

Thursday, October 17 (Moon in Aries) The moon is in your twelfth house today. Take time to reflect and meditate. Focus on remaining in the present moment, on being rather than doing. Think carefully before you act. There's a tendency now to undo all the positive actions you've taken. Avoid any self-destructive behavior. Be aware of hidden enemies.

Friday, October 18 (Moon in Aries)   There's a lunar eclipse in your twelfth house today. You could have an emotional reaction to a matter that arises from your past. Ultimately you gain better insight into that event. Unconscious attitudes can be difficult. Keep your feelings secret. It's a good day to work behind the scenes and observe from a distance.

Saturday, October 19 (Moon into Taurus, 2:28 a.m.) You get a fresh start, a new beginning today with the moon in your sign on a number 1 day. Your feelings and thoughts are aligned. Trust your hunches. Stress originality. It's all about your health and your emotional self: how you feel and how you feel about yourself.

Sunday, October 20 (Moon in Taurus)   The moon is on your ascendant today. The way you see yourself now is the way others see you. You're physically vital, and relations with the opposite sex go well. Your appearance and personality shine.

Monday, October 21 (Moon into Gemini, 11:15 a.m.)   Mercury goes retrograde in your seventh house today and stays there until November 10. During the next three weeks you could be feeling somewhat uncertain or insecure about your ability to communicate effectively. Expect some confusion in your communication with others, especially a romantic partner. You could also butt heads over a contract with a business partner. If possible, delay signing any contracts until Mercury goes direct.

Tuesday, October 22 (Moon in Gemini)   Whatever you value or your values play an important role in your day. With the moon in your second house today, Taurus, you can expect emotional experiences related to finances. You may be dealing with payments and collecting what's owed to you. You equate your financial assets with emotional security now. Look at your priorities in handling your income.

Wednesday, October 23 (Moon into Cancer, 10:37 p.m.)   Freedom of thought and action is key. It's a good day to promote new ideas. Approach the day with an unconventional mindset. You're versatile and changeable. Be careful not to spread out and diversify too much.

Thursday, October 24 (Moon in Cancer)   The moon is in your third house today. Trust your hunches. Express yourself dynamically, but control your emotions, especially in discussions with female relatives, siblings, and neighbors. Take what you know, and share it with others, especially those with creative minds.

Friday, October 25 (Moon in Cancer)   You're intuitive and nurturing today, but you could feel moody and overly sensitive. Take plenty of breaks from your work. That will help you clear your head and improve

211

your focus when you return to work. You feel best in your home environment.

Saturday, October 26 (Moon into Leo, 11:13 a.m.) It's a number 8 day, your power day and your day to play it your way. Expect a financial coup. Open your mind to a new approach that will pay off. You have a chance to expand, to gain recognition, fame, power. You attract financial success.

Sunday, October 27 (Moon in Leo)   The moon is in your fourth house today. It's a good day to stick close to home. Spend time with your family and other loved ones. But also find time to focus inward in quiet meditation. You feel a close tie to your roots. You could be dealing with your parents now.

Monday, October 28 (Moon into Virgo, 10:45 p.m.) You're at the top of your cycle again. It's a great time for initiating new projects, launching new ideas, or brainstorming. You take the lead on something new as you get a fresh start. In romance something new could be developing; a flirtation could turn more serious.

Tuesday, October 29 (Moon in Virgo)   The moon is in your fifth house today. Your emotions tend to overpower your intellect, but you're in touch with your creative side now. You also might be more possessive of loved ones and protective of children. Animals play a larger role than usual.

Wednesday, October 30 (Moon in Virgo)   Take care of details now, especially related to your health.

Exercise, and watch your diet. Stop worrying and fretting. Take time to write in a journal. You write from a deep place with lots of details and colorful descriptions. Dig deep for information.

Thursday, October 31 (Moon into Libra, 7:22 a.m.)
It's a number 4 day. Control your impulses, stay grounded today. Romance takes a back burner. Take care of your obligations. Remain focused, and you can solve any problem you face.

NOVEMBER 2013

Friday, November 1 (Moon in Libra) You could be interested in changing your diet and taking better care of yourself. Visit a health food store and stock up on herbs and vegetables. Take a yoga class, relax and stretch, release the stress. Or take a trip to the gym and challenge yourself to a vigorous workout.

Saturday, November 2 (Moon into Scorpio, 1:35 p.m.)
It's number 3 day. That means you're creative and express yourself well. Intuition is highlighted. Overall, the social energy of the day is warm and welcoming. Spread your good news, and take time to listen to others.

Sunday, November 3—Daylight Saving Time Ends (Moon in Scorpio) There's a solar eclipse today in your seventh house. That means new opportunities come your way that could involve a partner or a contract. With four planets also in Scorpio, everything is enhanced—for better or worse—especially your relationships with those close to you. It's the beginning or end of something.

Monday, November 4 (Moon into Sagittarius, 3:14 p.m.)   Variety is the spice of life. You're seeking new horizons. Think outside the box. Take risks, experiment. Get ready for changes. You can multitask efficiently today.

Tuesday, November 5 (Moon in Sagittarius)   Venus moves into your ninth house today. It's a great month for long-distance travel. In fact, you might fall in love on a journey. You could also get an article, story, or manuscript published. It's a good month for following your creative urges.

Wednesday, November 6 (Moon into Capricorn, 4:44 p.m.)   It's another mystery day, Taurus. Get ready for a journey into the unknown. Secrets, intrigue, confidential information play a role. Knowledge is essential to success. Gather information, but don't make any absolute decisions until tomorrow. You work best on your own today.

Thursday, November 7 (Moon in Capricorn)   With Jupiter going direct in your third house today, you're feeling optimistic and spiritually inclined. You get along well with your siblings and other relatives, and you benefit from those relationships. You can also expand any pursuits in education, communication, writing, and publishing.

Friday, November 8 (Moon into Aquarius, 6:31 p.m.)
It's a number 9 day. It's about beginnings and endings. Finish whatever you've been working on, and get ready for something new. Look for a new approach, a new perspective. The old cycle is ending, a new one about to begin. Visualize the future; set your goals, then make them so.

Saturday, November 9 (Moon in Aquarius)   The moon is in your tenth house of career today. Stay focused on professional concerns, and avoid emotional displays in public. You gain a boost in prestige, but be careful about mixing your business and professional lives.

Sunday, November 10 (Moon into Pisces, 9:37 p.m.)
Mercury goes direct in your seventh house today. Any confusion, miscommunication, and delays related to a partnership or contracts recede into the past. Things move more smoothly now. You get your message across, and everything works better, including computers and other electronic equipment.

Monday, November 11 (Moon in Pisces)   The moon is in your eleventh house today. You have deeper contact with friends now and could join a group of like-minded individuals. Social consciousness plays a role. You work for the common good, but keep an eye on your own wishes and dreams.

Tuesday, November 12 (Moon in Pisces)   Universal knowledge, eternal truths, deep spirituality are the themes of the day. Keep track of your dreams, including your daydreams. Ideas are ripe. You can tap deeply into the collective unconscious for inspiration. It's a day for deep healing.

Wednesday, November 13 (Moon into Aries, 2:40 a.m.)   Neptune goes direct in your eleventh house today. You have a strong spiritual need to pursue your wishes and dreams. You find it helpful to spend time in meditation, the deeper the better. You could be facing fears that have arisen related to a group activity. Friends play a role. You have considerable compassion for people who are down on their luck, outcasts of society.

Thursday, November 14 (Moon in Aries)   The moon is in your twelfth house today. It's a good day to work behind the scenes and avoid public scrutiny. You've had enough of that lately. Unconscious attitudes can be difficult and could relate to the past and your childhood. It's a good day to pursue a spiritual or mystical discipline.

Friday, November 15 (Moon into Taurus, 9:50 a.m.)
It's a number 7 day. You investigate, analyze, or simply observe what's going on now. You quickly come to a conclusion and wonder why others don't see what you see. You detect deception and recognize insincerity with ease. Express your desires, but avoid self-deception.

Saturday, November 16 (Moon in Taurus)   You're sensitive to other people's feelings. You may feel moody one moment, happy the next, then withdrawn and sad. It's all about your emotional self. Your feelings and thoughts are aligned.

Sunday, November 17 (Moon into Gemini, 7:08 p.m.)
There's a full moon in your first house today. You gain a new perspective on yourself and your emotions. Your appearance and personality shine. Your face is before the public. It's a time of harvest, a time of completion.

Monday, November 18 (Moon in Gemini) The moon is in your second house today. Expect emotional experiences related to money. Put off making any major purchases now. You feel best when surrounded by familiar objects in your home environment. It's not the objects themselves that are important, but the feelings and memories you associate with them.

Tuesday, November 19 (Moon in Gemini) It's a good day to express yourself in writing. You're feeling restless today and sending text messages to friends and associates to pass the time. You might be completing tasks faster than others do, and they could have trouble keeping up with you.

Wednesday, November 20 (Moon into Cancer, 6:24 a.m.) Your attitude determines everything. You communicate well. You're warm and receptive to what others say. You're creative and express yourself well. You will find that if you allow yourself free time, to fill in whatever silly or creative way you desire, then your spirits will soar, as will your productivity.

Thursday, November 21 (Moon in Cancer) The moon is in your third house today. A short trip works to your benefit now. Your mental abilities are strong, and you have an emotional need to reinvigorate your studies, especially regarding matters of the past. You're attracted to historical or archaeological subjects.

Friday, November 22 (Moon into Leo, 6:57 p.m.)
Change and variety are highlighted now. Think freedom, no restrictions. Release old structures; get a new point of view. It's a good day to take a risk, experiment. Promote new ideas. Find a new outlook that fits current circumstances and what you know.

Saturday, November 23 (Moon in Leo) The moon is in your fourth house today. You're dealing with the foundations of who you are and who you are becoming. Spend time with your family and other loved ones. Retreat to a private place for meditation. It's a good day for dream recall.

Sunday, November 24 (Moon in Leo) You're at center stage today. Theatrics and drama are highlighted. You're creative and passionate. It's a good day to dress up. Be wild, imaginative; be the person you always imagined you might be. Play with different personae.

Monday, November 25 (Moon into Virgo, 7:11 a.m.)
It's a number 8 day, your power day. Open your mind to a new approach. Unexpected resources arrive. You can go far with your plans and achieve financial success. But be aware that you're playing with power, so try not to hurt anyone.

Tuesday, November 26 (Moon in Virgo)   The moon is in your fifth house today. Be yourself now; be emotionally honest. Follow your heart related to a creative pursuit or relationship. Your emotions tend to overpower your intellect. It's an especially good day for pursuing a creative project or spending time with children.

Wednesday, November 27 (Moon into Libra, 5:00 p.m.)   It's a number 1 day. You're inventive and make connections that others overlook. You're determined and courageous today. Stress originality. In romance something new is developing. A flirtation turns more serious. Explore, discover, create.

Thursday, November 28 (Moon in Libra)   The moon is in your sixth house today. People are depending on you, and that can be a burden. Stop worrying— you're better off than you might think. You're restless and looking for change in your daily routine. A new job could be in store. Take care of any health issues now. Happy Thanksgiving.

Friday, November 29 (Moon into Scorpio, 11:04 p.m.) It's a number 3 day. You communicate well now. You're curious and inventive; ideas bubble forth. Your imagination is keen. Your popularity is on the rise.

Saturday, November 30 (Moon in Scorpio)   With the moon in your seventh house today, lovers and partners are highlighted. Your emotions are more intense. Women play a prominent role in your day. You feel a need to be accepted. You're looking for security, but you have a hard time going with the flow. A legal matter comes to a head now.

DECEMBER 2013

Sunday, December 1 (Moon in Scorpio)   With the moon in your seventh house today, the emphasis is on partnerships, marriage, and contracts. Women play a prominent role in your day. You get along well with others; you can fit in just about anywhere. Just be careful that no one manipulates your feeling.

Monday, December 2 (Moon into Sagittarius, 1:32 a.m.)   There's a new moon in your eighth house, indicating new opportunities come your way related to your career. You're moving into an intuitive flow today. You're also more open and accessible, but take care to avoid emotional displays, especially in public.

Tuesday, December 3 (Moon in Sagittarius)   The moon is in your eighth house today. You attract the attention of powerful people. You could be dealing with a matter related to shared belongings, investments, or taxes. An interest in metaphysics plays a role. You could be reading about concepts of life after death or reincarnation. Be aware that your experiences could be more intense than usual.

Wednesday, December 4 (Moon into Capricorn, 1:51 a.m.)   Mercury moves into your eighth house today. You're busy communicating with a partner and others about a mortgage, insurance, taxes, or an investment. Alternately, you could be telling someone close to you your ideas about life after death or other metaphysical matters.

Thursday, December 5 (Moon in Capricorn)   The moon is in your ninth house today. It's a good day to plan a long trip or sign up for a workshop or seminar. You're a dreamer and a thinker, Taurus. But you're also well grounded. You have an interest in philosophy, mythology, religion. You're feeling restless, looking for change. A foreign country or foreign-born person could play a role.

Friday, December 6 (Moon into Aquarius, 1:55 a.m.)
It's a number 2 day. It's all about cooperation and partnership. Show your appreciation to others. Help comes through friends and loved ones. Use your intuition to get a sense of your day. Be kind and understanding.

Saturday, December 7 (Moon in Aquarius)   Mars moves into your sixth house today. You're taking a more aggressive attitude about health issues. You're ready for a good workout at the gym. You might also commit yourself to a new diet. You have enough energy to help others, but you're not likely to allow them to manipulate you.

Sunday, December 8 (Moon into Pisces, 3:35 a.m.)
It's a number 1 day. You get a fresh start, a new beginning. Be independent and creative. Don't let others tell you what to do. Get out and meet new people, have new experiences, do something you've never done before. Express your opinions dynamically.

Monday, December 9 (Moon in Pisces) The moon is in your eleventh house today. You find meaning through friends and groups. You have deeper contact with friends now and could join a group of like-minded individuals. Work for the common good, but keep an eye on your own wishes and dreams.

Tuesday, December 10 (Moon into Aries, 8:06 a.m.) It's a number 3 day. You're innovative and creative and communicate well. You can influence people now with your upbeat attitude. Your artistic talents are highlighted. Ease up on your routines, and spread your good news. Your charm and wit are appreciated. Remain flexible.

Wednesday, December 11 (Moon in Aries) The moon is in your twelfth house today. It's a good day to withdraw and work behind the scenes. It's best to hide your emotions and moodiness. Avoid stubbornness and any self-destructive behavior. Things concerning the past and your childhood play a role.

Thursday, December 12 (Moon into Taurus, 3:41 p.m.) Change and variety are highlighted now. Release old structures; get a new point of view. Promote new ideas; follow your curiosity. Look for adventure, especially with a spouse or partner. You're courageous and adaptable today and, as always, well grounded, Taurus. It's a good time to pursue self-employment.

Friday, December 13 (Moon in Taurus) The moon is on your ascendant today. The way you see yourself now is the way others see you. Your appearance and personality shine. You're recharged for the rest of the month, and this makes you more appealing to the public. You're physically vital, and relations with the opposite sex go well.

Saturday, December 14 (Moon in Taurus) It's a good day to cultivate new ideas, but make sure to use common sense and take a down-to-earth perspective. Health and physical activity are highlighted. You're dealing with your emotional self, the person you are becoming.

Sunday, December 15 (Moon into Gemini, 1:41 a.m.) It's a number 8 day, a good day to buy a lotto ticket. It's your power day, your day to play it your way. You can go far with your plans and achieve financial success. Unexpected money comes your way.

Monday, December 16 (Moon in Gemini) Money and material goods are important to you now and give you a sense of security. You identify emotionally with your possessions or whatever you value. Put off making any major purchases. Look at your priorities in handling your income.

Tuesday, December 17 (Moon into Cancer, 1:17 p.m.) With Uranus going direct in your twelfth house today, you feel a strong need to work behind the scenes. You want to be on your own, but be careful not to isolate yourself. Avoid any self-destructive tendencies. Be aware of hidden enemies. There's also a full moon in your second house, which suggests that you reap what you've sown related to money matters.

Wednesday, December 18 (Moon in Cancer)   The moon is in your third house today. Take what you know, and share it with others. Communicate your ideas to siblings, other relatives, or neighbors. Try not to get overly emotional when making your point. It's a good day for writing in a journal.

Thursday, December 19 (Moon in Cancer)   You could feel moody today and overly sensitive. It's a good day to stay home and work on a project to beautify your home. Take time to relax and meditate. Tend to loved ones, do something with your children or sweetheart.

Friday, December 20 (Moon into Leo, 1:48 a.m.) It's time to get organized. Tear down the old in order to rebuild. Be methodical and thorough. Control your impulses. Stay focused, and persevere to get things done.

Saturday, December 21 (Moon in Leo)   Venus goes retrograde in your ninth house today and stays there until January 31. You could be facing some delays related to your travel plans or higher education. You may be somewhat uncomfortable dealing with someone from another country. Use this time to examine your feelings and your overall goals. Make sure those goals are an expression of who you are.

Sunday, December 22 (Moon into Virgo, 2:20 p.m.) It's a number 6 day. A change in the home, an adjustment or readjustment, is needed now. Don't put off the situation. That will only aggravate the problem. Be understanding, and avoid confrontations. Focus on making people happy. You offer advice and support. Be sympathetic and kind, generous and tolerant.

Monday, December 23 (Moon in Virgo) The moon is in your fifth house today. You feel a sudden surge of inspiration, a creative urge that helps you break through a block. In romance there's more depth and understanding in a relationship. Children play an important role in your day.

Tuesday, December 24 (Moon in Virgo) Mercury moves into your ninth house today. It's a great time to communicate your ideas at work. You yearn for a new experience. You move ahead quickly with plans related to foreign travel or higher education. Foreigners or a foreign country plays a role.

Wednesday, December 25 (Moon into Libra, 1:18 a.m.) Finish what you've started. Visualize the future; set your goals, then make them so. Clear up odds and ends. Take an inventory on where things are going in your life. It's a good day to make a donation to a worthy cause. Merry Christmas!

Thursday, December 26 (Moon in Libra) The moon is in your sixth house today. It's a service day. Others rely on you for help. You improve, edit, and refine their work. Help them, but don't deny your own needs. Take care of any health-care issues.

Friday, December 27 (Moon into Scorpio, 8:59 a.m.) It's a number 2 day. Partnerships play an important role. Cooperation is highlighted. Use your intuition to get a sense of your day. Be kind and understanding, especially to someone who is annoying you.

Saturday, December 28 (Moon in Scorpio)   The moon is in your seventh house today. The focus turns to relationships, business and personal ones. You get along well with others now. You can fit in just about anywhere. Loved ones and partners are more important than usual. A legal matter comes to your attention.

Sunday, December 29 (Moon into Sagittarius, 12:38 p.m.)   It's a number 4 day. Put your organizational skills to use. Revise and rewrite. Tear down in order to rebuild. Be methodical and thorough. Stay focused, and emphasize quality. You're in the right place at the right time.

Monday, December 30 (Moon in Sagittarius)   The moon is in your eighth house today. If you are planning on making a major purchase, make sure that you and your partner are in agreement. Otherwise you could encounter intense emotional resistance. An interest in metaphysics plays a role in your day. You could be dealing with a mystery of the unknown.

Tuesday, December 31 (Moon into Capricorn, 1:02 p.m.)   It's a service day. You offer advice and support. Be diplomatic, kind, and understanding. Avoid scattering your energies. If you're going out tonight to a New Year's Eve party, you might volunteer to be the designated driver.

HAPPY NEW YEAR!

Wednesday, January 1 (Moon in Capricorn) The year begins with a new moon and five planets in your ninth house of higher mind, higher education and travel. That means new opportunities come your way today and throughout the month related to a long-distance trip, pursuing higher education, or exploring the higher mind. You could get a chance to study in a foreign land, or a foreign-born person plays a significant role in your life this month. Look for a new beginning on this New Year's Day.

Thursday, January 2 (Moon into Aquarius, 12:04 p.m.) You're creative and express yourself well today. Your artistic talents are highlighted. Enjoy the harmony, beauty, and pleasures of life. Beautify your home. Overall, the social energy of the day is warm and welcoming.

Friday, January 3 (Moon in Aquarius) The moon is in your tenth house today. Focus on your professional concerns. You could be dealing with bosses and others in power. You can be more responsive to the needs and moods of others around you now. A word of caution, Taurus: An office romance could be dangerous.

Saturday, January 4 (Moon into Pisces, 11:59 a.m.) You're versatile and changeable now, but be careful not to spread yourself too thin. Release old structures; get a new point of view. Take a risk; experiment. Approach the day with an unconventional mindset.

Sunday, January 5 (Moon in Pisces)   The moon is in your eleventh house today. Friends play an important role in your day, especially Virgo and Capricorn. You find strength in numbers. You find meaning through friends and groups, especially a group of like-minded people working for the common good.

Monday, January 6 (Moon into Aries, 2:46 p.m.) It's a number 7 day. You work best on your own today. Knowledge is essential to success. Gather information, but don't make any absolute decisions until tomorrow. Go with the flow. Secrets or intrigue could play a role in your day. You investigate, analyze, or simply observe what's going on.

Tuesday, January 7 (Moon in Aries)   The moon is in your twelfth house today. Think carefully before you act or speak. Consider: Is it kind, is it true, is it necessary? If you're not careful, there's a tendency now to undo all the positive actions you've taken. You might feel a need to withdraw. Take time to reflect and meditate.

Wednesday, January 8 (Moon into Taurus, 9:24 p.m.) Finish what you started, Taurus, and get ready for something new. But don't start anything today. Look beyond the immediate. Visualize the future; set your goals, then make them so. Express your desires, but avoid self-deception. Maintain your emotional balance.

Thursday, January 9 (Moon in Taurus)   The moon is on your ascendant today, Taurus. The way you see yourself now is the way others see you. You're recharged for the rest of the month, and this makes you more appealing to the public. You're physically vital, and relations with the opposite sex go well. You're sensitive to other people's feelings.

Friday, January 10 (Moon in Taurus)   Under the influence of the Taurus moon, health and physical activity are highlighted. Be aware that you might be somewhat stubborn and resistant to change. It's a good day to use common sense and take a down-to-earth perspective on whatever you're doing.

Saturday, January 11 (Moon into Gemini, 7:26 a.m.) Mercury moves into your tenth house until January 31. You can use your speaking and writing abilities this month to move ahead in your profession. You get along well with others in the workplace, but you don't feel any strong emotional attachments at this time. You can work out a new strategy now to advance your career.

Sunday, January 12 (Moon in Gemini)   The moon is in your second house today. There could be some emotional discussions related to money now. Watch your spending. You feel a sense of security, Taurus, by surrounding yourself with the things that have meaning for you. It's not the objects themselves that are important, but the feelings and memories you associate with them.

Monday, January 13 (Moon into Cancer, 7:25 p.m.)
It's a number 5 day. Change is highlighted now. Variety is the spice of life. Think outside the box. Take risks; experiment. You're versatile and changeable, but be careful not to diversify too much.

Tuesday, January 14 (Moon in Cancer)   The moon is in your third house today. You get your ideas across as you go about your everyday activities. Take what you've learned recently, and tell others about it. But avoid getting overly emotional, especially when dealing with neighbors or relatives.

Wednesday, January 15 (Moon in Cancer)   There's a full moon in your third house today with Saturn forming a beneficial angle. You reap what you've sown now related to your everyday world. You communicate well and get your message across. You're more serious and responsible in dealing with others in your community, neighborhood, or extended family. That's not a passing theme, but one that will remain with you for months to come.

Thursday, January 16 (Moon into Leo, 8:01 a.m.)
It's a number 8 day. That means you attract financial success now. You're playing with power, so be careful not to hurt others. You can go far with your plans and achieve financial success. Business discussions go well.

Friday, January 17 (Moon in Leo)   The moon is in your fourth house today. Family matters play a big role. You're dealing with the foundations of who you are. Spend time with family and loved ones. Decide together how you're going to beautify your home.

Saturday, January 18 (Moon into Virgo, 8:25 p.m.) You're at the top of your cycle today, Taurus. You get a fresh start now, a new beginning. Be independent and creative, and refuse to be discouraged by naysayers. You can take the lead on a new project. You're determined and courageous.

Sunday, January 19 (Moon in Virgo)   With the moon in your fifth house today, you're emotionally in touch with your creative side, Taurus. There's also greater depth in a love relationship and more involvement with any children or pets in your life. Make sure that you're not overly protective of children. They need room to grow.

Monday, January 20 (Moon in Virgo)   Under the influence of the Virgo moon, you may exhibit some perfectionist tendencies. Take care of details, especially related to your health. Exercise and watch your diet. Stop worrying and fretting. Take time to write in a journal. You write from a deep place now with lots of details and colorful descriptions.

Tuesday, January 21 (Moon into Libra, 7:45 a.m.) It's a number 4 day. Your organizational skills are highlighted. Control your impulses. Set aside romantic notions for the time being. Persevere and fulfill your obligations. You're building foundations for your creativity. Emphasize quality.

Wednesday, January 22 (Moon in Libra)   The moon is in your sixth house today. It's a service-oriented day, Taurus. Help others, but be careful not to fall into a martyr syndrome. Don't let your fears hold you back. Also, attend to details related to your health. Make a doctor or dentist appointment.

Thursday, January 23 (Moon into Scorpio, 4:45 p.m.) It's another service-oriented day. You're well grounded, Taurus, and offer advice and support to those around you. Do a good deed for someone. Be sympathetic and kind, generous and tolerant. Diplomacy wins the way. An adjustment in your domestic life may be necessary now.

Friday, January 24 (Moon in Scorpio)   The moon is in your seventh house today. The focus turns to relationships, business and personal ones. You get along well with others. You can fit in just about anywhere. Loved ones and partners are more important than usual.

Saturday, January 25 (Moon into Sagittarius, 10:14 p.m.)   It's your power day today, Taurus, and your day to play it your way. Unexpected money arrives. You can go far with your plans and achieve financial success. It's a good day to buy a lotto ticket. You pull off a financial coup. Be courageous; be yourself. People in power are watching.

Sunday, January 26 (Moon in Sagittarius)   The moon is in your eighth house today. You attract powerful people to you. Your experiences could be intense, especially related to income or belongings that you share with someone. An interest in metaphysics plays a role.

Monday, January 27 (Moon in Sagittarius)   Under the influence of the Sag moon, you have an opportunity to expand and grow. Look to the big picture as you focus on who you are and what you're doing. Luck comes your way today.

Tuesday, January 28 (Moon into Capricorn, 12:05 a.m.)   It's a number 2 day. Partnerships play an important role in your day. Cooperation is highlighted. Use your intuition to get a sense of your day. Be kind and understanding.

Wednesday, January 29 (Moon into Aquarius, 11:33 p.m.)   You're creative and express yourself well today. Your artistic talents are highlighted. Remain flexible. Your intuition is highlighted. Spread your good news. Ease up on routines. It's all about balance and creativity.

Thursday, January 30 (Moon in Aquarius)   There's a new moon in your tenth house today. New opportunities come to the forefront as you are rewarded for a job well done. Business dealings are highlighted. You're more responsive to the needs and moods of a group or of the public in general. With Uranus forming a beneficial angle, whatever happens now shakes you out of a rut or an old routine. You embrace what's new and different.

Friday, January 31 (Moon into Pisces, 10:45 p.m.)
Mercury moves into your eleventh house today. You
communicate well with others, especially friends or a
group of like-minded people. You can now clarify
your wishes and dreams by either talking to a close
friend or writing in a journal. With Venus going direct
in your ninth house, you love the idea of pursuing
higher education or planning a long trip.

FEBRUARY 2014

Saturday, February 1 (Moon in Pisces) The
moon is in your eleventh house today. Friends play an
important role in your day. You work well with a
group of like-minded individuals. At the same time,
you pursue your wishes and dreams.

Sunday, February 2 (Moon into Aries, 11:55 p.m.)
It's a number 4 day. Take care of your obligations. Get
everything in order. Tear down the old in order to rebuild. Be methodical and thorough. You're building
foundations for an outlet for your creativity. Emphasize quality.

Monday, February 3 (Moon in Aries) With the
moon in your twelfth house today, you tend to withdraw from public view, Taurus. Unconscious attitudes
can be difficult now. So can relations with women.
Keep your feelings secret. Work behind the scenes,
and follow your intuition.

Tuesday, February 4 (Moon in Aries) Under the
influence of the Aries moon, you get powered up for

the rest of the month. It's a great day to brainstorm. You come up with new ideas. You're passionate but impatient. You're in the public eye and very persuasive, especially if you're passionate about what you're doing.

Wednesday, February 5 (Moon into Taurus, 4:47 a.m.) It's your mystery day, Taurus. You investigate, analyze, or simply observe what's going on now. You quickly come to a conclusion and wonder why others don't see what you see. You detect deception and recognize insincerity with ease.

Thursday, February 6 (Moon in Taurus) Mercury turns retrograde in your eleventh house, where it stays until February 28. That means you can expect delays and glitches related to your wishes and dreams. There could be confusion related to your involvement in a group. Don't worry; it will all work out by early next month.

Friday, February 7 (Moon into Gemini, 1:45 p.m.) It's a number 9 day. Visualize the future; set your goals, then make them so. Complete a project, clear up odds and ends. Take an inventory on where things are going in your life. It's a good day to make a donation to a worthy cause.

Saturday, February 8 (Moon in Gemini) The moon is in your second house today. Money and material goods are important to you and give you a sense of security. You identify emotionally with your possessions or whatever you value. You may be dealing with payments and collecting what's owed to you. Look at your priorities in handling your income.

Sunday, February 9 (Moon in Gemini)   Under the influence of the Gemini moon, you're feeling restless today and contacting friends to pass the time. Your mind moves quickly from one thought to another. It's a good day for a change of scenery, such as a short trip to visit relatives or friends. Get out and socialize.

Monday, February 10 (Moon into Cancer, 1:34 a.m.) You're warm and receptive to what others say. Your imagination is keen now. You're curious and inventive. Enjoy the harmony, beauty, and pleasures of life. You have a strong sense of duty and feel obligated to fulfill your promises.

Tuesday, February 11 (Moon in Cancer)   The moon is in your third house today. Your communications with others are subjective. Take what you know, and share it. However, keep conscious control of your emotions when communicating. Your thinking is unduly influenced by things of the past.

Wednesday, February 12 (Moon into Leo, 2:17 p.m.) It's a number 5 day. That means you're open to change and variety, and you desire to loosen any restrictions today. You're willing to take a risk and experiment. Variety is the spice of life, and change is good. Think outside the box.

Thursday, February 13 (Moon in Leo)   The moon is in your fourth house today. Take time to work on a home-repair project that you've been ignoring. A parent plays a role in your day. You're dealing with the foundations of who you are and who you are becoming. You feel a close tie to your roots.

Friday, February 14 (Moon in Leo)   There's a full moon in your fourth house, which suggests that you reap what you've sown related to domestic matters. You gain insight into plans to renovate your home or your home life. Take your sweetheart out to dinner. Happy Valentine's Day.

Saturday, February 15 (Moon into Virgo, 2:27 a.m.) It's a number 8 day, your power day. Take a chance; buy a lotto ticket. Expect a big bonus, a financial windfall. Unexpected money comes your way. Business dealing go well, especially if you open your mind to a new approach.

Sunday, February 16 (Moon in Virgo)   With the moon in your fifth house today, it's a good day to take a chance, experiment. Be aware that your emotions tend to overpower your intellect. You're emotionally in touch with your creative side. Alternately, you are more protective and nurturing toward children.

Monday, February 17 (Moon into Libra, 1:24 p.m.) It's a number 1 day, so you're at the top of your cycle. It's a great time for initiating new projects, launching new ideas, or brainstorming for new ways of making money. You take the lead on something new as you get a fresh start. Follow your heart.

Tuesday, February 18 (Moon in Libra)   With the moon in your sixth house today, the emphasis turns to your daily work and service to others. Attend to all the details. Be careful not to overlook any seemingly minor matters that could take on importance. Keep up with your exercise plan, and watch your diet.

Wednesday, February 19 (Moon into Scorpio, 10:33 p.m.)   Take time to relax, enjoy yourself, recharge your batteries. Have fun today in preparation for tomorrow's discipline and focus. Remain flexible in your schedule. Foster generosity.

Thursday, February 20 (Moon in Scorpio)   The moon is in your seventh house today. You get along well with others now. You can fit in just about anywhere. Loved ones and partners are more important than usual. You comprehend the nuances of a situation, but it's difficult to go with the flow. Be careful that others don't manipulate your feelings.

Friday, February 21 (Moon in Scorpio)   Under the influence of the Scorpio moon, you're more passionate than usual. Your sexuality is heightened. Investigate, research, and dig deep. Be aware of things happening in secret and of possible deception. But forgive and forget; try to avoid going to extremes.

Saturday, February 22 (Moon into Sagittarius, 5:12 a.m.)   Focus on making people happy. You offer advice and support. Be sympathetic and kind, generous and tolerant. Diplomacy wins the way. Be understanding, and avoid confrontations. Dance to your own tune.

Sunday, February 23 (Moon in Sagittarius)   With the moon in your eighth house, Taurus, you could attract power people to you today. Your energy is more intense than usual, and drama plays a role. Your emotions could affect your feelings about belongings that you share with others. An interest in metaphysics or related rituals grabs your attention.

Monday, February 24 (Moon into Capricorn, 8:51 a.m.)   It's a number 8 day. Business discussions go well. Unexpected money arrives. You're in the power seat, Taurus, so focus on a power play. Be aware that you're playing with power, so try not to hurt anyone. Be courageous. Be yourself; be honest.

Tuesday, February 25 (Moon in Capricorn)   The moon is in your ninth house today, the home of higher learning. You're full of ideas on matters such as philosophy or religion, the law or publishing. You also have a strong interest in foreign travel or a foreign nation. It's a good time to look to the big picture, Taurus. Break away from your routine or the usual way you think about things.

Wednesday, February 26 (Moon into Aquarius, 9:56 a.m.)   You're at the top of your cycle again, Taurus. You get a fresh start, a new beginning. Get out and meet new people, have new experiences, do something you've never done before. You're inventive and

239

make connections that others overlook. Stress originality.

Thursday, February 27 (Moon in Aquarius)   The moon is in your tenth house today. You gain recognition for what you do. You're in the public eye. You get along well with fellow workers and are much admired. You have a strong desire for high achievement through hard work, and others respect your efforts.

Friday, February 28 (Moon into Pisces, 9:53 a.m.) Mercury goes direct in your tenth house. Confusion, miscommunication, and delays related to your professional life recede into the past. Things move more smoothly. You get along with others better, and you get your message across. Everything works better, including computers and other electronic equipment.

MARCH 2014

Saturday, March 1 (Moon in Pisces)   There's a new moon in your eleventh house, which means new opportunities come your way related to your association with a group working for a common cause. Meanwhile, Mars turns retrograde in your sixth house, where it stays until May 19. That suggests any aggressive actions you take in the workplace will be met by delays and confusion. With Neptune forming a favorable conjunction, it's a good time for writing or reading works of fiction.

Sunday, March 2 (Moon into Aries, 10:41 a.m.) Saturn turns retrograde in your seventh house today.

You'll be thinking more about partnerships and contracts. By the time Saturn goes direct again July 20, you should be able to better integrate the responsibility of each partner into your life. Release old structures; get a new point of view.

Monday, March 3 (Moon in Aries) The moon is in your twelfth house today. Think carefully before you act. There's a tendency now to undo all the positive actions you've taken. You feel best working behind the scenes. Avoid any self-destructive behavior. Be aware of hidden enemies.

Tuesday, March 4 (Moon into Taurus, 2:13 p.m.) It's a number 7 day. You pursue a mystery now. Gather information, but don't make any absolute decisions until tomorrow. Go with the flow. Maintain emotional balance, and avoid confusion and conflict.

Wednesday, March 5 (Moon in Taurus) Venus moves into your tenth house today. The next four weeks are a great time for your career development. Other people are very receptive to you, especially bosses and peers. You could win recognition, a raise, an award.

Thursday, March 6 (Moon into Gemini, 9:39 p.m.) Jupiter goes direct in your third house today. You're very competent and resourceful handling everyday activities. You're busy keeping your mind occupied with new information and looking for ways to expand whatever you're doing. For better or worse, your thinking is unduly influenced by things of the past.

Friday, March 7 (Moon in Gemini)   The moon is in your second house today. So it's a good day for dealing with money issues. Pay what you owe, and collect what others owe you. You equate your financial assets with emotional security now. Look at your priorities in handling your income.

Saturday, March 8 (Moon in Gemini)   Under the influence of the Gemini moon, you're feeling restless today and contacting friends to pass the time. Your mind moves quickly from one thought to another. It's a good day for a change of scenery, such as a short trip to visit relatives or friends. Get out and socialize.

Sunday, March 9—Daylight Saving Time Begins (Moon into Cancer, 9:34 a.m.)   It's a number 3 day. You're warm and receptive to what others say. Your imagination is keen now. You're curious and inventive. Enjoy the harmony, beauty, and pleasures of life. You have a strong sense of duty and feel obligated to fulfill your promises.

Monday, March 10 (Moon in Cancer)   The moon is in your third house today. Your mental abilities are strong, and you have an emotional need to reinvigorate your studies, especially regarding matters of the past. Take what you know and share it with others, but stay in control of your emotions, especially when dealing with siblings, other relatives, or neighbors.

Tuesday, March 11 (Moon into Leo, 10:10 p.m.) You're restless and looking for change, a new perspective. You're versatile and changeable, but be careful not to overcommit yourself now. Stay focused as best you can. Take risks; experiment. Pursue a new idea. Freedom of thought and action is key.

Wednesday, March 12 (Moon in Leo)   The moon is in your fourth house. You're dealing with foundations, the very foundations of who you are and who you are becoming. Make an effort to change a bad habit. It's best today to work on your own. Spend time with your family and other loved ones; work on a project to beautify your home.

Thursday, March 13 (Moon in Leo)   Under the influence of the Leo moon, your feelings are more intense than usual today, and there's high drama in the air as security becomes an important issue for you. Your sense of duty and obligation can affect your feelings about shared belongings. Matters of sex, death and rebirth, rituals, and relationships emerge.

Friday, March 14 (Moon into Virgo, 10:18 a.m.)
It's a number 8 day, your power day, and you're in the power seat. You have a chance to expand, to gain recognition, even fame and power. Open your mind to a new approach. You pull off a financial coup. Unexpected money arrives.

Saturday, March 15 (Moon in Virgo)   The moon is in your fifth house today. It's a great day for pursuing a creative project. Your emotions tend to overpower your intellect. Be yourself; be emotionally honest. In love there's greater emotional depth to a relationship. In business dealings diversify now. Insist on all the details, not just bits and pieces.

Sunday, March 16 (Moon into Libra, 8:46 p.m.)
There's a full moon in your fifth house today. You gain insight and illumination related to a relationship, especially during the morning hours. It could be a time of completion or a new beginning, related to romance or a creative project. Any children in your life play an important role.

Monday, March 17 (Moon in Libra) Mercury moves into your eleventh house today. You work well with a group, expressing your ideas. You're friendly but impersonal in your dealings with others. Your thoughts tend to be somewhat quirky now and so are some of your friends, who provide you with a variety of ideas.

Tuesday, March 18 (Moon in Libra) The moon is in your sixth house today. Don't let your fears hold you back. Help others, but don't deny your own needs. Visit someone who is ill, but don't forget about your own health needs. Keep up with your exercise plan, and watch your diet.

Wednesday, March 19 (Moon into Scorpio, 5:14 a.m.)
It's a number 4 day. Your organizational skills are highlighted. Control your impulses. Persevere to get things done today, and don't get sloppy. Tear down the old in order to rebuild. Be methodical and thorough. Revise, rewrite.

Thursday, March 20 (Moon in Scorpio) The moon is in your seventh house today. Cooperation is highlighted. Don't make waves; just go with the flow. Loved ones and partners are more important than usual. A contract could play a role.

Friday, March 21 (Moon into Sagittarius, 11:39 a.m.) It's a number 6 day. Focus on making people happy today. Service to others is the theme of the day. You offer advice and support. Visit someone who is ill or in need of help.

Saturday, March 22 (Moon in Sagittarius) The moon is in your eighth house today. Your sense of security or duty plays a major role in your day. You help others, especially a partner. You could be managing another person's money or an inheritance. You're dealing with mortgages, taxes, or insurance. Alternately, you're attracted to the goals of a large social movement.

Sunday, March 23 (Moon into Capricorn, 4:04 p.m.) It's a number 8 day, your power day, so focus on a power play. You can go far with your plans and achieve financial success. Open your mind to a new approach that could bring in big bucks. It's a good day to buy a lotto ticket.

Monday, March 24 (Moon in Capricorn) The moon is in your ninth house today. You may feel a need to get away now, a break from the usual routine. You yearn for a new experience. Foreigners or a foreign country plays a role in your day. It's a good time to plan a long trip or sign up for a workshop or seminar.

Tuesday, March 25 (Moon into Aquarius, 6:40 p.m.)
It's a number 1 day, and you're at the top of your cycle again. You're determined and courageous today. Stress originality in whatever you're doing. Refuse to deal with people who have closed minds. Explore, discover, create. In romance something new could be brewing. A flirtation turns more serious.

Wednesday, March 26 (Moon in Aquarius)   The moon is in your tenth house today, and that means professional concerns take priority. After your positive day yesterday, you could gain favor from bosses or the public. It's a good day for sales and dealing with the public. You're more responsive to the needs of others, especially coworkers.

Thursday, March 27 (Moon into Pisces, 8:12 p.m.)
Your disposition determines everything today. You can influence people with your upbeat attitude. Spread your good news. Ease up on routines. Your charm and wit are appreciated. In romance you're an ardent and loyal lover.

Friday, March 28 (Moon in Pisces)   The moon is in your eleventh house today. Friends play an important role in your day, especially Virgo and Capricorn. You work well with a group now, but don't overlook your own goals. Focus on your wishes and dreams, and make sure that they remain an expression of who you are.

Saturday, March 29 (Moon into Aries, 9:55 p.m.)
It's a number 5 day. Freedom of thought and action is key now. Variety is the spice of life. Take risks; experiment. Approach the day with an unconventional mindset. You're surprisingly versatile and changeable today, Taurus.

Sunday, March 30 (Moon in Aries)   There's a new moon in your twelfth house. That means new opportunities come your way related to something hidden from public view. You work best behind the scenes. With Uranus closely conjunct, you can expect sudden and unexpected changes as a matter from the past surfaces. The key to dealing with the situation is self-control.

Monday, March 31 (Moon in Aries)   The moon is on your ascendant today. You're recharged for the month ahead. The way you see yourself now is the way others see you. Your face is in front of the public. Your appearance and personality shine. You're dealing with your emotional self, the person you are becoming.

APRIL 2014

Tuesday, April 1 (Moon into Taurus, 1:21 a.m.)
It's a number 5 day. Promote new ideas; follow your curiosity. Freedom of thought and action is key. A change of scenery would do you good. You're versatile and changeable. However, be careful not to spread out and diversify too much.

Wednesday, April 2 (Moon in Taurus)   The moon is on your ascendant today. You get recharged for the month ahead, and this make you more appealing to the public. You're physically vital, and relations with the opposite sex go well. The way you see yourself now is the way others see you. Your thoughts and feelings are aligned.

Thursday, April 3 (Moon into Gemini, 7:49 a.m.) It's your mystery day, Taurus. You launch a journey into the unknown. You become aware of confidential information, secret meetings, things happening behind closed doors. You investigate like a detective solving a mystery. Dig deep, gather information, but don't act on what you learn until tomorrow.

Friday, April 4 (Moon in Gemini)   The moon is in your second house today. You identify emotionally with your possessions or whatever you value. It's not the objects themselves that are important, but the feelings and memories you associate with them. Look at your priorities in handling your income. Put off making any major purchases.

Saturday, April 5 (Moon into Cancer, 5:40 p.m.) Venus moves into your eleventh house today. You put others at ease now in social situations. You benefit from friends and social contacts and work smoothly with a group, especially if you're dealing with something artistic and creative.

Sunday, April 6 (Moon in Cancer)   The moon is in your third house today. You're busy interacting with neighbors, relatives, or siblings in a social gathering. You get your ideas across, but try not to get too emotional. A female relative plays an important role.

Monday, April 7 (Moon in Cancer) Mercury moves into your twelfth house, where it stays until April 23. It's a good time to work behind the scenes and avoid any conflict. You could be dealing with a matter from the past that has returned to haunt you. Keep your feelings secret. Follow your intuition. You confide your thoughts and ideas to a close friend.

Tuesday, April 8 (Moon into Leo, 5:51 a.m.) It's a number 3 day. Your attitude determines everything today, Taurus. Spread your good news. You're innovative and creative and communicate well. But you're also well grounded. Enjoy the harmony, beauty, and pleasures of life.

Wednesday, April 9 (Moon in Leo) The moon is in your fourth house today. Spend time with your family and loved ones. Stick close to home, if possible. A parent plays a role in your day. Work on a home-repair project; beautify your surroundings.

Thursday, April 10 (Moon into Virgo, 6:08 p.m.) Change and variety are highlighted now. Think freedom; think outside the box. No restrictions. Your creativity, personal grace, and magnetism are highlighted.

Friday, April 11 (Moon in Virgo) With the moon in your fifth house, yesterday's energy flows into your Friday. You're emotionally in touch with your creative side. You also might be more involved with kids. Animals play a role in your day. It's a good day to take a chance, experiment. Be emotionally honest.

Saturday, April 12 (Moon in Virgo)   Under the influence of the Virgo moon, it's a good time to take care of details, especially related to a contract or partnership. Stop worrying and fretting. Dig deep for information. Take time to write in a journal. You write from a deep place now with lots of details and colorful descriptions. Remember to exercise and watch your diet.

Sunday, April 13 (Moon into Libra, 4:34 a.m.) It's a number 8 day, your power day. Business discussions go well. You attract financial success. Open your mind to a new approach that could bring in big bucks. You have a chance to expand, to gain recognition, even fame and power.

Monday, April 14 (Moon in Libra)   Pluto goes retrograde in your ninth house today, where it stays until September 22. You take a deeper look at your worldview, your spiritual beliefs. There could be some profound inner changes coming in your life.

Tuesday, April 15 (Moon into Scorpio, 12:21 p.m.) There's a lunar eclipse in your sixth house today. You have an emotional reaction to a development in the workplace, or it could be related to a health issue. With Mars forming a positive angle, whatever happens provides you with new energy and works to your advantage.

Wednesday, April 16 (Moon in Scorpio)   The moon is in your seventh house today. Partnerships play a key role in your day. You tend to get along well with others, especially someone with whom you share possessions or income. You comprehend the nuances of a situation, but it's difficult to remain detached and objective now. Be careful that others don't manipulate your feelings.

Thursday, April 17 (Moon into Sagittarius, 5:44 p.m.) It's a number 3 day. Everything eases up now. The intensity you've been feeling evaporates. Be happy, positive, upbeat. Your attitude determines everything. You're well liked and receive a social invitation. Your charm and wit are appreciated. Spend time in conversation. Hobbies are accented.

Friday, April 18 (Moon in Sagittarius)   The moon is in your eighth house today. Your experiences are more intense than usual. You could be dealing with a relationship matter that involves your possessions or shared belongings. Alternately, an interest in metaphysical subjects, such as life after death or reincarnation, plays a role in your day.

Saturday, April 19 (Moon into Capricorn, 9:29 p.m.) Approach your day with an unconventional mindset. Let go of old structures; get a new point of view. Change and variety are highlighted now. Think outside the box. Take risks; experiment.

Sunday, April 20 (Moon in Capricorn)   The moon is in your ninth house today. That means it's a good time to start thinking about a long trip. Make your plans now. You're feeling restless. It's also a good time to explore ideas, philosophies, mythology. You're a dreamer and thinker. A friend could introduce you to someone new and exciting from far away.

Monday, April 21 (Moon in Capricorn) Under the influence of the Capricorn moon, your ambition and drive to succeed are highlighted. Your responsibilities increase. You may feel stressed, overworked. Authority figures, elderly people play a role. Be conservative; don't speculate or take any unnecessary risks.

Tuesday, April 22 (Moon into Aquarius, 12:19 a.m.) It's a number 8 day, your power day and your day to play it your way. Open your mind to a new approach, and a windfall may come your way. You attract financial success. Keep in mind that you're playing with power, so be careful not to hurt others.

Wednesday, April 23 (Moon in Aquarius) Mercury moves into your first house today, where it stays until May 7. You're very chatty and expanding your network of contacts. Your ideas reflect your personality. You're quick and witty now and easily adapt to changing circumstances.

Thursday, April 24 (Moon into Pisces, 2:56 a.m.) You're at the top of your cycle again. You get a fresh start, a new beginning. In romance make room for a new love. A flirtation turns more serious. Explore and discover. Creativity is highlighted. Express your opinions dynamically.

Friday, April 25 (Moon in Pisces)   The moon is in your eleventh house today. You get along better with friends and associates. You work for the common good, but keep an eye on your own wishes and dreams. Make sure that they remain an expression of who you are.

Saturday, April 26 (Moon into Aries, 6:02 a.m.) Take time to relax, enjoy yourself, recharge your batteries. You can influence people now with your upbeat attitude. Your charm and wit are appreciated. Foster generosity. In romance you're an ardent and loyal lover.

Sunday, April 27 (Moon in Aries)   The moon is in your twelfth house today. It's a good day to work behind the scenes and avoid any conflict. You could be dealing with a matter from the past that has returned to haunt you. Keep your feelings secret. Follow your intuition.

Monday, April 28 (Moon into Taurus, 10:24 a.m.) It's a number 5 day. Change and variety are highlighted now. Approach the day with an unconventional mindset, a new perspective. Take a risk. Think outside the box. Promote new ideas; follow your curiosity. A change of scenery would work to your advantage.

Tuesday, April 29 (Moon in Taurus)   There's a solar eclipse in your first house today. That means new opportunities affecting your personal life are knocking. Whatever is coming will benefit you in a major way. With Mercury forming a favorable angle, you communicate your ideas well, and they help you move ahead and take advantage of the opportunities.

Wednesday, April 30 (Moon into Gemini, 4:56 p.m.)
It's a number 7 day, a mystery day. Knowledge is essential to success. You investigate, analyze, or simply observe what's going on now. Look behind closed doors. Confidential information could be involved. But don't make any absolute decisions until tomorrow. Go with the flow.

MAY 2014

Thursday, May 1 (Moon in Gemini) The moon is in your second house today. That means money issues are on the table. Pay what you owe, and collect what others owe you. You equate your financial assets with emotional security now. Look at your priorities in handling your income.

Friday, May 2 (Moon in Gemini) With Venus moving into your twelfth house today, you could be dealing with a secret affair, a romance behind the scenes, or a longing for someone committed to another person. There could be heartbreak, guilt, or shame involved, especially if the other person is not free.

Saturday, May 3 (Moon into Cancer, 2:13 a.m.)
It's your power day. You attract financial success.

Open your mind to a new approach that could bring in big bucks. Be aware, though, that fear of failure or fear that you won't measure up will attract tangible experiences that reinforce the feeling.

Sunday, May 4 (Moon in Cancer) The moon is in your third house today. You're busy keeping your mind occupied with new information. Your communications with others are subjective. Take what you know, and share it with others. However, keep conscious control of your emotions when communicating. Your thinking is unduly influenced by a matter from the past.

Monday, May 5 (Moon into Leo, 1:56 p.m.) It's a number 1 day, and you're at the top of your cycle. You're inventive and make connections that others overlook. You're determined and courageous today. You can take the lead now and get a fresh start, a new beginning. Don't be afraid to shift directions if that feels right for you now. Trust your hunches; intuition is highlighted.

Tuesday, May 6 (Moon in Leo) The moon is in the house of the home today. It's a good day to spend time with your family and other loved ones. A parent could be involved in your day. You feel grounded and close to your roots, Taurus. See if you can remember a dream from last night.

Wednesday, May 7 (Moon in Leo) Mercury moves into your second house today. There's lots of mental stimulation now regarding finances. You discuss ideas about making money. You're analytical about it rather than passionate. Values are important to you now, but they tend to be material rather than moral.

Thursday, May 8 (Moon into Virgo, 2:25 a.m.)   It's a number 4 day. Your organizational skills are called upon. You're building foundations for the future, developing outlets for your creativity. Emphasize quality in whatever you're doing. Be methodical and thorough.

Friday, May 9 (Moon in Virgo)   The moon is in your fifth house today. It's a great day for pursuing a creative project. Children play a role in your day. Your emotions tend to overpower your intellect. Be yourself; be emotionally honest. In love there's greater emotional depth to a relationship now. Sex for pleasure is highlighted.

Saturday, May 10 (Moon into Libra, 1:20 p.m.) It's a number 6 day. Service to others is the theme of the day. Offer advice and support. Be sympathetic and tolerant. Focus on making people happy. Diplomacy wins the way.

Sunday, May 11 (Moon in Libra)   With the moon in your sixth house today, yesterday's energy flows into your Sunday. It's another service-oriented day. You're the one others go to for help now. Offer your assistance, but know when to say enough is enough. Don't fall into a martyr syndrome, and don't let your fears hold you back. You improve, edit, and refine the work of others.

Monday, May 12 (Moon into Scorpio, 9:08 p.m.) You're in the power seat. More money comes your way from a financial venture. You can go far with your plans and achieve financial success. You have a chance to expand, to gain recognition, fame, power.

Tuesday, May 13 (Moon in Scorpio) The moon is in your seventh house today. You get along well with others. You can fit in just about anywhere. Loved ones and partners are more important than usual. Take time to consider how others see you. You're in the public eye.

Wednesday, May 14 (Moon in Scorpio) There's a full moon in your seventh house today. That means yesterday's energy flows into your Wednesday. Now you can reap what you've sown related to a partnership. With Saturn closely conjunct, a partnership is taken to a deeper level of commitment. You're more serious about a relationship.

Thursday, May 15 (Moon into Sagittarius, 1:45 a.m.) It's a number 2 day. Cooperation is highlighted. Use your intuition to get a sense of the day. Don't make waves. Don't rush or show resentment. Let things develop. The spotlight is on cooperation. Show your appreciation to others.

Friday, May 16 (Moon in Sagittarius) The moon is in your eighth house today. An interest in metaphysics plays a role in your day. So do sex, death, rebirth, rituals, and relationships. You could take an interest in exploring life after death. Alternately, mat-

257

ters involving mortgages, insurance, taxes, or investments could arise.

Saturday, May 17 (Moon into Capricorn, 4:13 a.m.)
It's a number 4 day. Persevere to get things done today. Don't get sloppy. Tear down the old in order to rebuild. Be methodical and thorough. Revise, rewrite. You're at the right place at the right time.

Sunday, May 18 (Moon in Capricorn)   The moon is in your ninth house today. Your mind is active, and you yearn for new experiences, a break from the routine, a change from the status quo. Your thoughts run wild. You're a dreamer and thinker, and your thoughts tend to rattle the status quo. You jump easily from one idea to another.

Monday, May 19 (Moon into Aquarius, 5:59 a.m.)
With Mars going direct in your sixth house today, Taurus, you tend to be more aggressive than usual in dealing with those who seek your help. If there's a meeting at work, you forcefully push your point of view. You challenge others and can be somewhat combative in your position. Alternately, you could be aggressively dealing with a health issue.

Tuesday, May 20 (Moon in Aquarius)   The moon is in your tenth house today. Business dealings are highlighted as you gain an elevation in prestige. Your life is more public. You're more emotional and warm toward coworkers, but avoid emotional displays in public.

Wednesday, May 21 (Moon into Pisces, 8:19 a.m.)
It's a number 8 day. It's your power day, your day to play it your way. Business discussions go well. You can go far with your plans and achieve financial success. However, be aware that you're playing with power, so try not to hurt anyone.

Thursday, May 22 (Moon in Pisces) The moon is in your eleventh house today. You find strength in numbers and meaning through friends and groups. You work for the common good, but keep an eye on your own wishes and dreams. Social consciousness plays a role.

Friday, May 23 (Moon into Aries, 12:02 p.m.)
You're at the top of your cycle again, Taurus. That means you get a fresh start, a new outlook. You can take the lead now, and don't be afraid to turn in a new direction. Express your opinions dynamically. In romance a flirtation turns more serious.

Saturday, May 24 (Moon in Aries) The moon is in your twelfth house today. It's a good day to withdraw and spend time in private; relax and meditate. Keep your feelings to yourself, unless you confide in a close friend. Follow your intuition. It's a great day for a mystical or spiritual discipline.

Sunday, May 25 (Moon into Taurus, 5:28 p.m.)
Spread your good news, and take time to listen to others. Ease up on routines. Your charm and wit are appreciated. You're innovative and creative and

communicate well. Your artistic talents are high-lighted. Enjoy the harmony, beauty, and pleasures of life.

Monday, May 26 (Moon in Taurus)   The moon is on your ascendant today. The way you see yourself now is the way others see you. Your thoughts and feelings are aligned. You're physically vital, and relations with the opposite sex go well. You're especially appealing to the public now.

Tuesday, May 27 (Moon in Taurus)   With the moon in your first house, Taurus, it's all about your health and your emotional self: how you feel and how you feel about yourself. Your feelings tend to fluctuate by the moment. You could spend time either procrastinating or changing your plans. You focus on how the public relates to you.

Wednesday, May 28 (Moon into Gemini, 12:48 a.m.)
Venus moves into your first house today. Others notice your personal grace and friendly outlook. Your presence is quite pleasing to others now. You're outgoing and making new friends. A note of advice: Guard against vanity. Meanwhile, there's a new moon in your second house. That means new money-making opportunities come your way. With Uranus forming a beneficial angle, positive changes in finances could happen fast, as if out of nowhere.

Thursday, May 29 (Moon in Gemini)   Who needs Starbucks? You've got Mercury in your third house. You're more witty and clever than usual. Your mind is stimulated; you're alert, adaptable, and versatile. However, be aware that after Mercury goes retrograde June 7, not everyone will appreciate that wit and wry humor.

Friday, May 30 (Moon into Cancer, 10:14 a.m.) It's a number 8 day, your power day. Open your mind to a new approach. Unexpected resources arrive. You can go far with your plans and achieve financial success. But be aware that you're playing with power, so try not to hurt anyone.

Saturday, May 31 (Moon in Cancer) The moon is in your third house today. You can be quite opinionated now, especially if you're talking with siblings, other family members, or neighbors. Try to stay in control of your emotions. You tend to be affected by matters from the past.

JUNE 2014

Sunday, June 1 (Moon into Leo, 9:44 p.m.) It's your mystery day, Taurus. You work best on your own today. Secrets, intrigue, confidential information play a role. You investigate, analyze, or simply observe what's going on now. You quickly come to a conclusion and wonder why others don't see what you see. You detect deception and recognize insincerity with ease. Maintain your emotional balance.

Monday, June 2 (Moon in Leo) The moon is in your fourth house today. It's a good day to work on a project to beautify your home. Your intuition is highlighted. Spend time with your family and other loved ones. But also find time to focus inward in quiet meditation.

Tuesday, June 3 (Moon in Leo)   Under the influence of the Leo moon, drama is highlighted, perhaps involving children. You're at center stage today. Dress boldly; showmanship is emphasized. You're creative and passionate, impulsive and honest. Romance feels majestic.

Wednesday, June 4 (Moon into Virgo, 10:21 a.m.) You're at the top of your cycle again, Taurus. You get a new beginning, a chance to prove yourself. Don't be afraid to take a risk by following a new path. Trust your hunches. Explore, discover, create. Refuse to deal with people with closed minds.

Thursday, June 5 (Moon in Virgo)   The moon is in your fifth house today. Your love life takes off. There's an idealistic turn to whatever you do for pleasure. It's a great time for a creative project, especially fiction writing. You could be somewhat possessive of loved ones and children. It's a good day to get a pet!

Friday, June 6 (Moon into Libra, 10:02 p.m.) Ease up on your routines, and spread your good news. You communicate well. You're warm and receptive to what others say. Your imagination is keen now; you're curious and inventive. Enjoy the harmony, beauty, and pleasures of life. Beautify your home.

Saturday, June 7 (Moon in Libra)   Mercury goes retrograde in your third house today, where it stays until July 1. That means you can expect some delays and glitches in communication over the next three weeks in your everyday life. When dealing with family members, especially siblings, or neighbors, make yourself clearly understood. There also could be delays related to short-distance travel. So leave enough time for your appointments.

Sunday, June 8 (Moon in Libra)   The moon is in your sixth house today. Others come to you for guidance. They rely on you for information. Provide help, but be careful not to fall into a martyr syndrome. Don't forget your own needs. Take care of any health issues. Take time to exercise, and watch your diet.

Monday, June 9 (Moon into Scorpio, 6:39 a.m.) Neptune goes retrograde in your eleventh house today. You're highly intuitive, but friends and associates might misunderstand your comments about your wishes and dreams. You could feel an urge to embrace a philosophy that is out of the ordinary, and that could cause some confusion among members of a group.

Tuesday, June 10 (Moon in Scorpio)   The moon is in your seventh house today. Relationships, business and personal ones, are on your mind. You get along well with others now and can fit in just about anywhere. Loved ones and partners are more important than usual. A legal matter comes to your attention.

Wednesday, June 11 (Moon into Sagittarius, 11:24 a.m.)   It's a number 8 day. Focus on a power play today. You can go far now and achieve financial success, especially if you try a new approach. Expect a windfall. Business discussions go well. Be courageous. Be yourself; be honest.

Thursday, June 12 (Moon in Sagittarius)   The moon is in your eighth house today. If you are planning on making a major purchase, make sure that you and your partner are in agreement. Otherwise you could encounter intense emotional resistance. An interest in metaphysics plays a role in your day. You could be dealing with a mystery of the unknown.

Friday, June 13 (Moon into Capricorn, 1:05 p.m.) There's a full moon in your eighth house today with Uranus forming a beneficial angle. That means you reap what you've sown related to shared finances. It could involve an inheritance, insurance, or taxes. You gain insight, and your dreams are vivid.

Saturday, June 14 (Moon in Capricorn)   The moon is in your ninth house today. You may feel a need to get away now, a break from the usual routine. Pursue a new idea. Follow your dreams. It's a good time to plan a long trip or take a meditation class to venture to inner worlds.

Sunday, June 15 (Moon into Aquarius, 1:28 p.m.) It's a number 3 day. You're innovative and creative and communicate well today, Taurus. Enjoy the harmony, beauty, and pleasures of life. Your attitude determines everything. Spread your good news, and take time to listen to others.

Monday, June 16 (Moon in Aquarius)   The moon is in your tenth house today. It's a good day for sales and dealing with the public. You gain an elevation in prestige related to your career. Business dealings are highlighted. You're warmer and friendlier toward co-workers, but don't make any emotional displays in public.

Tuesday, June 17 (Moon into Pisces, 2:26 p.m.) It's a number 5 day. Change and variety are highlighted now. Variety is the spice of life. Think outside the box. Take risks; experiment. Release old structures; get a new point of view.

Wednesday, June 18 (Moon in Pisces)   The moon is in your eleventh house today. Group activities are highlighted. You get along well with others, especially if you're working as a group for a common cause or goal. Take a look at your own goals, and make sure that they're still an expression of who you are.

Thursday, June 19 (Moon into Aries, 5:26 p.m.) It's your mystery day, Taurus. You work best on your own today. Secrets, intrigue, confidential information play a role. You investigate, analyze, or simply observe what's going on now. You quickly come to a conclusion and wonder why others don't see what you see. You detect deception and recognize insincerity with ease. Maintain your emotional balance.

Friday, June 20 (Moon in Aries)   The moon is in your twelfth house today. You communicate your deepest feelings to a trustworthy friend, but otherwise you keep your thoughts and feelings to yourself. You feel best now working behind the scenes. Take time to reflect and meditate.

Saturday, June 21 (Moon into Taurus, 11:03 p.m.) It's a good day to complete a project; clear up odds and ends. Don't start anything new today. Take an inventory on where things are going in your life. Strive for universal appeal.

Sunday, June 22 (Moon in Taurus)   It's all about your health and your emotional self now: how you feel and how you feel about yourself. You're malleable and easily change your mind today, restless and uncertain what to do. You are sensitive and responsive to the needs of others, so you're easily influenced by those around you.

Monday, June 23 (Moon in Taurus)   Venus moves into your second house today. It's a good day to bolster your finances. You can make money through the arts now, but watch your spending, Taurus. You could be feeling somewhat extravagant in your desire to purchase luxury items.

Tuesday, June 24 (Moon into Gemini, 7:06 a.m.) Others notice how grounded and steady you are, Taurus. Your charm and wit are appreciated today. Your imagination is keen now, and you communicate well.

You're warm and receptive to what others say. Your popularity is definitely on the rise.

Wednesday, June 25 (Moon in Gemini)   The moon is in your second house today. Expect emotional experiences related to money and your values. You seek financial and domestic security now, and you feel best surrounded by familiar objects. It's a good day for investments, but be practical. Don't make any major purchases.

Thursday, June 26 (Moon into Cancer, 5:06 p.m.) The emphasis is on freedom of thought and movement. Get ready for a change of scenery or a possible relocation. It's a good day to experiment and find a new outlook. You have the ability to stay grounded while making changes, Taurus. Variety is the spice of life.

Friday, June 27 (Moon in Cancer)   There's a new moon in your third house today. That means new opportunities come your way related to your everyday life. It's a doorway to something new. It could involve a neighbor, close family member, or other relative. You communicate your thoughts well.

Saturday, June 28 (Moon in Cancer)   Under the influence of the Cancer moon, your home and personal environment are important to you. You're intuitive and nurturing, but you also could feel moody today and overly sensitive. It might seem as if the world is out to get you. It's not. Take plenty of breaks from your work. That will help you clear your head and improve your focus.

Sunday, June 29 (Moon into Leo, 4:44 a.m.)   It's a number 8 day, your power day. Be courageous and take a chance. Buy a lotto ticket. Business dealings go well. Expect a financial coup. You have an opportunity today to expand, to gain recognition, even fame.

Monday, June 30 (Moon in Leo)   The moon is in your fourth house today. Pay more attention to the domestic scene. A parent plays a role. Work on a home-repair project, but take time to retreat to a private place for meditation.

JULY 2014

Tuesday, July 1 (Moon into Virgo, 5:25 p.m.)   Mercury goes direct in your second house today, where it stays until July 12. That means any confusion related to your communication with others ends, and delays related to local travel are over. New money-making ideas are on your mind, and you let others know. You could also be discussing your ideals or whatever you value.

Wednesday, July 2 (Moon in Virgo)   The moon is in your fifth house today. Your emotions tend to overpower your intellect. It's a good day to pursue a creative project. You feel strongly attached to loved ones, particularly children. Animals play a role in your day.

Thursday, July 3 (Moon in Virgo)   Under the influence of the Virgo moon, you could be exhibiting some perfectionist tendencies. Stick close to home; focus on tidying up the house, attending to the details and loose ends. But take time to relax and make a new entry in a personal journal. You write from a deep place now with lots of details and colorful descriptions.

Friday, July 4 (Moon into Libra, 5:44 a.m.)   Use your intuition to get a sense of your day. Be kind and understanding. Your intuition focuses on relationships, both personal and professional. Business dealings are highlighted. Don't make waves; the spotlight is on cooperation. Happy Independence Day!

Saturday, July 5 (Moon in Libra)   The moon is in your sixth house today. People are depending on you, and that can be a burden. Stop worrying. You're better off than you might think. You're restless and looking for change in your daily routine. A new job could be in store. Don't forget to exercise and watch your diet.

Sunday, July 6 (Moon into Scorpio, 3:34 p.m.) Persevere to get things done today. Take care of your obligations, and don't get sloppy. Put off any impulse to wander off task. You're building a foundation for the future.

Monday, July 7 (Moon in Scorpio)   The moon is in your seventh house today. A legal matter comes to your attention. You comprehend the nuances of a situation, but it's difficult to go with the flow. Be careful that others don't manipulate your feelings. A spouse or partner plays a major role in your day.

Tuesday, July 8 (Moon into Sagittarius, 9:25 p.m.)
It's a number 6 day. Diplomacy wins the way. Focus on making people happy; do a good deed. Be sympathetic and kind, generous and tolerant. But know when enough is enough. Avoid scattering your energies.

Wednesday, July 9 (Moon in Sagittarius) You're feeling as if you need to break out of your usual routine, or it could turn into a rut, Taurus. Travel or higher education plays a role. Plan a trip or sign up for a seminar or workshop. A foreign country or person of foreign birth could play a role.

Thursday, July 10 (Moon into Capricorn, 11:25 p.m.)
It's your power day, Taurus. Unexpected money arrives. Open your mind to a new approach that could bring in big bucks. Business discussions go well. You're being watched by people in power.

Friday, July 11 (Moon in Capricorn) The moon is in your ninth house today. You're a dreamer and thinker, and you yearn for new experiences. It's a great time to sign up for a workshop or seminar on a subject of interest. You could also follow your wanderlust and plan a long journey. Study and investigate possible destinations and sites along the way.

Saturday, July 12 (Moon into Aquarius, 11:07 p.m.)
Mercury is still direct in your third house today. That

means you communicate well with family members, especially siblings, as well as neighbors. Your mind is especially quick, and you make your point clearly. There's also a full moon in your ninth house, indicating that you reap what you've sown related to higher education or plans for long-distance travel.

Sunday, July 13 (Moon in Aquarius) The moon is in your tenth house today. You're either gaining a boost in your status and personal achievement, or you're feeling in need of such recognition. Fortunately you stay grounded, Taurus, no matter what happens. Others appreciate your persistence. You find yourself more in the public now, but try to avoid any overly emotional displays.

Monday, July 14 (Moon into Pisces, 10:41 p.m.) Take time to relax, enjoy yourself, recharge your batteries. You can influence people now with your upbeat attitude. Your charm and wit are appreciated. Foster generosity. In romance you're an ardent and loyal lover.

Tuesday, July 15 (Moon in Pisces) With the moon in your eleventh house today, you feel a need to withdraw and work behind the scenes. It's a great day for pursuing a spiritual discipline. There's a tendency now towards secrecy and difficult dealings with others, especially women.

Wednesday, July 16 (Moon in Pisces) Jupiter moves into your fourth house today. You have a good opportunity over the coming weeks and months to expand your home life. You could be building an addition onto your house or might be expanding your family. Alternately, you could develop or enlarge a home-based business.

Thursday, July 17 (Moon into Aries, 12:07 a.m.)
It's a number 6 day. Service to others is the theme of the day. Be sympathetic and kind, generous and tolerant. Do a good deed for someone. Visit someone who is ill or in need of help. An adjustment in your domestic life may be necessary now.

Friday, July 18 (Moon in Aries) Venus moves into your third house today. You're especially interested in pursuing cultural and artistic endeavors. It's a good day for working on an enjoyable writing project; your creativity is heightened. Music plays a role in your day. You get along well with family members, siblings, and neighbors.

Saturday, July 19 (Moon into Taurus, 4:43 a.m.)
It's a number 8 day, your power day. Focus on a power play. Business dealings go well. You can go far with your plans and achieve financial success. You're playing with power, so be careful not to hurt others. It's a good day to buy a lotto ticket.

Sunday, July 20 (Moon in Taurus) Saturn goes direct in your seventh house today. You're moving into a period of greater mental discipline and more structure to your thoughts, especially related to partnerships. The emphasis is on pursuing practical ideas and not taking chances. You could encounter some feelings of depression. Be particularly cautious in signing legal documents.

Monday, July 21 (Moon into Gemini, 12:37 p.m.)
Uranus goes retrograde in your twelfth house, and this could mean some erratic and unexpected developments related to your involvement with institutions such as hospitals or government offices. Best advice: try not to make mountains out of molehills. You may be looking deeply into your life and wondering how past events are affecting you. You could experience bursts of intuitive energy related to matters from the past.

Tuesday, July 22 (Moon in Gemini) The moon is in your second house today. Expect emotional experiences related to money. Money and material goods are important to you now and give you a sense of security. Look at your priorities in handling your income. Your values are important to you now, and so are the *things* that you value.

Wednesday, July 23 (Moon into Cancer, 11:00 p.m.)
It's a number 3 day. Your attitude determines everything today. You're innovative and creative and communicate well. You're also warm and receptive to others. Foster generosity. Take time to relax, enjoy yourself, recharge your batteries.

Thursday, July 24 (Moon in Cancer) The moon is in your third house today. You'll probably be running around, taking care of chores in your everyday world. You could hear from a sibling, other relative, or neighbor, and if so you can expect an invitation. Control your emotions when expressing any opinions, especially on matters related to the past.

Friday, July 25 (Moon in Cancer) With Mars in your seventh house, you should be aware that over the next six weeks problems might flare up related to a partner. It could be a business partner or your mate. Watch out for aggressive behavior on your part. You feel a need to be accepted. You're looking for security, but you tend to try to force the issue.

Saturday, July 26 (Moon into Leo, 10:56 a.m.) There's a new moon in your fourth house today, and that means new opportunities come your way related to your home. If you're selling your home now, you could get an offer. With Jupiter forming a nice angle, you could also have an opportunity to pursue or expand a home-based business.

Sunday, July 27 (Moon in Leo) Under the influence of the Leo moon, you're creative and passionate today. Drama is highlighted, perhaps involving children. Romance feels majestic. Dress boldly; showmanship is emphasized.

Monday, July 28 (Moon into Virgo, 11:37 p.m.) It's a number 8 day, your power day and your day to do it your way. You're in the power seat, so look for a power play. You have a chance to expand, to gain recognition, even fame and power. Be courageous. Be yourself; be honest.

Tuesday, July 29 (Moon in Virgo) With the moon in your fifth house today, it's a good day to experiment with something new. Your creativity is emphasized. Your originality is highlighted. Be aware that your emotions tend to overpower your intellect. Alternately, you are more protective and nurturing toward children.

Wednesday, July 30 (Moon in Virgo) Under the influence of the Virgo moon, you feel an urge to help others. You also can dig deep for information as you search for details, especially related to your health. Stop worrying and fretting. Take time to exercise, and watch your diet.

Thursday, July 31 (Moon into Libra, 12:10 p.m.) It's a number 2 day. Don't make waves. Don't rush or show resentment; let things develop. Cooperation is highlighted. Use your intuition to get a sense of your day. Be kind and understanding.

AUGUST 2014

Friday, August 1 (Moon in Libra) The moon is in your sixth house today. Your personal health occupies your attention now. Keep your resolutions about exercise, and watch your diet. Attend to details related to making a doctor or dentist appointment. Help others, but don't deny your own needs.

Saturday, August 2 (Moon into Scorpio, 10:57 p.m.) You're at the top of your cycle, Taurus. It's your turn to take the lead. Others see you as well grounded. Be independent and creative, and don't deal with people with closed minds. You get a fresh start. Stress originality. In romance something new is developing.

Sunday, August 3 (Moon in Scorpio)   The moon is in your seventh house today as the focus turns to partnerships, personal and business. A legal matter could be involved. Women play a prominent role. You get along well with others now, but be careful that they don't manipulate your feelings.

Monday, August 4 (Moon in Scorpio)   Under the influence of the Scorpio moon, you're more passionate than usual. Your sexuality is heightened. Investigate, research, and dig deep. Be aware of things happening in secret and of possible deception. But forgive and forget; try to avoid going to extremes.

Tuesday, August 5 (Moon into Sagittarius, 6:19 a.m.) Get organized now. Clean out a closet or straighten up your desk. Keep your goals in mind; follow your ideas. Be tenacious. You tend to stay with the tried and true. It's not a day for experimentation or new approaches.

Wednesday, August 6 (Moon in Sagittarius)   The moon is in your eighth house today. You're interested in exploring a metaphysical matter, such as life after death or reincarnation. Your intuition is strong. But you have to deal with more mundane issues, such as insurance, taxes, or credit card payments. You also could be managing resources that you share with others.

Thursday, August 7 (Moon into Capricorn, 9:39 a.m.)
Service to others is the theme of the day. You offer
advice and support. Be sympathetic and kind, generous and tolerant. Focus on making people happy. Diplomacy wins the way. Your persistence is recognized.

Friday, August 8 (Moon in Capricorn)   With the
moon in your ninth house today, you're playing with
ideas that could involve a foreign destination or a person of foreign origin. A long trip or higher education
plays a role. You have an interest in ideas, mythology,
or philosophy.

Saturday, August 9 (Moon into Aquarius, 9:53 a.m.)
It's your power day. So focus on a power play. You
can go far with your plans and achieve financial success. It's a good day to buy a lotto ticket. Expect a
windfall.

Sunday, August 10 (Moon in Aquarius)   There's
a full moon in your tenth house today, suggesting that
you reap what you've sown related to your career
goals. With Uranus forming a beneficial angle, you
gain sudden insight related to your career. You could
be inspired to ask for a raise or advancement.

Monday, August 11 (Moon into Pisces, 8:56 a.m.)
You're at the top of your cycle again. Get out and
meet new people, have new experiences, do something you've never done before. You're inventive and
make connections that others overlook. You get a
fresh start now. Trust your hunches.

Tuesday, August 12 (Moon in Pisces)   Venus moves into your fourth house today. That indicates that any artistic or creative pursuits in the home prosper. It's a good day to work on a home-repair project that's a labor of love.

Wednesday, August 13 (Moon into Aries, 9:01 a.m.) You're warm and receptive to what others say. Your imagination is keen now; you're curious and inventive. Enjoy the harmony, beauty, and pleasures of life, Taurus. You have a strong sense of duty and feel obligated to fulfill your promises.

Thursday, August 14 (Moon in Aries)   With the moon in your twelfth house today, you communicate your deepest feelings to another person. With others, it's best to keep your feelings secret. Be aware that unconscious attitudes can be difficult now. So can relations with women. It's a good day to work behind the scenes and follow your intuition.

Friday, August 15 (Moon into Taurus, 11:59 a.m.) Mercury moves into your fifth house today, Taurus. You're feeling creative, and you communicate your thoughts well. Others see you as witty and clever. In romance you're likely to talk about issues that have arisen.

Saturday, August 16 (Moon in Taurus)   With the moon in your first house today, your self-awareness and appearance are important. You're dealing with the person you are becoming. It's all about your health and emotional self now: how you feel and how you feel about yourself. You're sensitive and responsive to the needs of others, so you're easily influenced by those around you.

Sunday, August 17 (Moon into Gemini, 6:42 p.m.)
It's your mystery day, a number 7 day, Taurus. That means you launch a journey into the unknown. You look behind closed doors. You investigate and dig deep. Your native persistence pays off. Secrets and confidential information could play a role. Stay balanced and grounded, and don't react.

Monday, August 18 (Moon in Gemini) The moon is in your second house today. Expect emotional experiences related to money and your values. You have the opportunity now to reevaluate your situation and make important changes. You communicate your ideas about your values in life. You have a better understanding of what your values are. Stay grounded, Taurus.

Tuesday, August 19 (Moon in Gemini) Under the influence of the Gemini moon, your mind is moving quickly today. You get your ideas across and are busy sending messages or talking on the phone. You're looking for intellectual stimulation, but you tend to analyze and rationalize too much. Have a party, socialize, get out and have fun; flirt.

Wednesday, August 20 (Moon into Cancer, 4:46 a.m.)
It's a number 1 day. You get a fresh start and a new beginning. Don't be afraid to turn in a new direction. Trust your hunches. Get out and meet new people,

have new experiences, do something you've never done before. Explore, discover; creativity is highlighted. Express your opinions dynamically.

Thursday, August 21 (Moon in Cancer) The moon is in your third house today. While you communicate well with immediate family, other relatives, and neighbors, you tend to get emotional, especially if you're dealing with matters from the past. Take care if you're driving and talking on your cell. Eyes on the road, hands on the wheel.

Friday, August 22 (Moon into Leo, 4:50 p.m.) Ease up on your routines, Taurus. Your attitude determines everything today. Take time to relax, enjoy yourself, recharge your batteries. You can influence people now with your upbeat attitude.

Saturday, August 23 (Moon in Leo) The moon is in your fourth house today. You're dealing with the foundations of who you are and who you are becoming. Retreat to a private place for meditation. It's a good day for dream recall. It's best to work on your own and stay focused. You can eliminate a bad habit.

Sunday, August 24 (Moon in Leo) Under the influence of the Leo moon, you're creative and passionate today. Drama is highlighted, perhaps involving children. Romance feels majestic. Dress boldly; showmanship is emphasized.

Monday, August 25 (Moon into Virgo, 5:33 a.m.) There's a new moon in your fifth house today. That means you get new opportunities related to a creative project. A doorway opens. It's a good time to begin a new project that's aimed at helping others. Alternately, a romance takes on new life.

Tuesday, August 26 (Moon in Virgo) Under the influence of the Virgo moon, you're more open today to helping others who might be rivals at other times. You also can dig deep for information as you search for details, especially related to your health. Stop worrying and fretting. Take time to exercise, and watch your diet.

Wednesday, August 27 (Moon into Libra, 5:54 p.m.) It's a number 8 day, another power day, so focus on a power play. Open your mind to a new approach that could bring in big bucks. Think big and act big. However, remember that you're playing with power, so be careful not to hurt others. You attract financial success, recognition, and even fame.

Thursday, August 28 (Moon in Libra) The moon is in your sixth house today. It's a service day. Help others, but don't deny your own needs. Keep your resolutions about exercise, and watch your diet. Your personal health occupies your attention now.

Friday, August 29 (Moon in Libra) Under the influence of the Libra moon, you find yourself in a position to settle a dispute. You seek harmony and peace. Your creativity, personal grace, and magnetism play a role. You're also looking for balance as you fine-tune a love relationship.

Saturday, August 30 (Moon into Scorpio, 4:53 a.m.)
It's a number 2 day. The spotlight is on cooperative efforts and partnerships. Be kind and understanding, patient and supportive. Let things develop. Don't make waves; don't rush or show resentment.

Sunday, August 31 (Moon in Scorpio) The moon is in your seventh house today. The focus turns to partnerships. Under the Scorpio moon, be careful how you deal with disagreements. Any conflict will be more emotional than usual. However, it's difficult to remain detached and objective.

SEPTEMBER 2014

Monday, September 1 (Moon into Sagittarius, 1:17 p.m.) You're at the top of your cycle as the month begins. Be independent and creative, and refuse to be discouraged by naysayers. You're inventive and make connections that others overlook. You're determined and courageous today.

Tuesday, September 2 (Moon in Sagittarius) Mercury moves into your sixth house today. You efficiently handle your duties and communicate well with others. Health and diet play a role, but don't get compulsive about it. You work best now with a clean desk. Disorder upsets you.

Wednesday, September 3 (Moon into Capricorn, 6:16 p.m.) Take time to relax, enjoy yourself, recharge your batteries. You can influence people now with your upbeat attitude. Your charm and wit are appreciated. Foster generosity. In romance you're an ardent and loyal lover.

Thursday, September 4 (Moon in Capricorn)   The moon is in your ninth house today. You're a dreamer and thinker, and you yearn for new experiences. It's a great time to sign up for a workshop or seminar on a subject of interest. You could also follow your wanderlust and plan a long journey. Study and investigate possible destinations and sites along the way.

Friday, September 5 (Moon into Aquarius, 8:00 p.m.)
It's a number 5 day for you. Release old structures; get a new point of view, a change in perspective. Freedom of thought and action is key. Promote new ideas; follow your curiosity.

Saturday, September 6 (Moon in Aquarius)   The moon is in your tenth house today. You communicate your feelings well to coworkers, who are sympathetic. You get along well with others in the workplace. Your life is more public now, but take care to avoid overt emotional displays.

Sunday, September 7 (Moon into Pisces, 7:48 p.m.)
It's a number 7 day. You work best on your own today as you journey into the unknown. Secrets, intrigue, confidential information play a role. You investigate, analyze, or simply observe what's going on now. Gather information, but don't make any absolute decisions until tomorrow.

Monday, September 8 (Moon in Pisces) There's
a full moon in your eleventh house today. That means
a time of completion related to a group activity. You
find strength in numbers. You find fulfillment through
friends and groups, and your goals are achieved now
through their help. With Saturn forming a beneficial
angle, whatever you hear about is a serious matter.
Saturn also brings more structure into your life and
allows you to take advantage of what you've learned.

Tuesday, September 9 (Moon into Aries, 7:34 p.m.)
It's a number 9 day. That means it's time to complete
a project. Clear your desk and make room for the new,
but don't start anything until tomorrow. Spend some
time in deep thought. Consider how you can expand
your base.

Wednesday, September 10 (Moon in Aries) The
moon is in your twelfth house today. It's a good day to
work behind the scenes and avoid any conflict. You
could be dealing with a matter from the past that has
returned to haunt you. Keep your feelings secret. Follow your intuition.

**Thursday, September 11 (Moon into Taurus, 9:17
p.m.)** It's a number 2 day. The spotlight is on cooperation. Try to avoid stubborn behavior when others question your actions. Don't make waves. Don't
rush or show resentment; let things develop. Show
your appreciation to others.

Friday, September 12 (Moon in Taurus) The
moon is on your ascendant today. Your face is in front

of the public. You focus on self-awareness, your appearance, and the person you are becoming. Your feelings and thoughts are aligned. You're physically vital, and relations with the opposite sex go well.

Saturday, September 13 (Moon in Taurus)   With Mars moving into your eighth house today, you're an investigator and a problem solver. You dig deep for information in whatever area that interests you or is of greatest importance. Your sex drive is strong now. However, tension could arise in any dealings related to joint resources or an inheritance.

Sunday, September 14 (Moon into Gemini, 2:27 a.m.)   It's a number 5 day. You're restless and looking for change, a new perspective. You're versatile and changeable, but be careful not to overcommit yourself now. Stay focused as best you can. Take risks; experiment. Pursue a new idea. Freedom of thought and action is key.

Monday, September 15 (Moon in Gemini)   With the moon in your second house, money issues surface. You could get a quick financial boost today. It's a good time for investments. Look at your priorities in spending your income. Take care of payments and collections.

Tuesday, September 16 (Moon into Cancer, 11:24 a.m.)   It's your mystery day, Taurus. You become aware of confidential information, secret meetings, things happening behind closed doors. You investigate like a detective solving a mystery. Gather information, but don't act on what you learn until tomorrow.

Wednesday, September 17 (Moon in Cancer)   The moon is in your third house today. Your mental abilities are strong, and you have an emotional need to reinvigorate your studies, especially regarding matters of the past. You're attracted to historical studies or prehistorical explorations. Take what you know, and share it with others. You could be getting involved in a challenging mental activity, such as on-line gaming, a debate, or a game of chess.

Thursday, September 18 (Moon into Leo, 11:10 p.m.)
Visualize your future by setting your goals. Look beyond the immediate, and make room for something new. Complete a project, and clear up odds and ends. Take an inventory on where things are going in your life, Taurus. Let go of any stubborn behavior, and change what needs to be changed.

Friday, September 19 (Moon in Leo)   With the moon in your fourth house today, it's a good day to spend time with your family and other loved ones. Stick close to home. You're dealing with the foundations of who you are and who you are becoming. Retreat to a private place for meditation. See if you can remember your dreams from last night.

Saturday, September 20 (Moon in Leo)   Under the influence of the Leo moon, you're at center stage today. You like to flaunt and celebrate. Be wild, imaginative; be the person you always imagined you might be. Play with different personae. You're creative and passionate.

Sunday, September 21 (Moon into Virgo, 11:54 a.m.)
It's a number 3 day. Your charm and wit are appreciated today. Your imagination is keen; you're curious and inventive. You communicate well, and you're warm and receptive to what others say.

Monday, September 22 (Moon in Virgo)　Pluto goes direct in your ninth house today. You feel very attached to your ideas about religion, philosophy, or mythology. You'll cling to these ideas or concepts for years. At the same time there could be some tension with those around you over the way you think about higher education or travel to foreign lands. Be aware of power struggles, and see if you can diffuse them before they get out of control.

Tuesday, September 23 (Moon in Virgo)　The moon is in your fifth house today. Your love life takes off. There's an idealistic turn to whatever you do for pleasure. It's a great time for a creative project, especially fiction writing. You could be somewhat possessive of loved ones and children. It's a good day to get a pet!

Wednesday, September 24 (Moon into Libra, midnight)　There's a new moon in your sixth house today, and that means new opportunities come your way related to your daily work. It's a good time to get rid of a bad habit, Taurus, and possibly start on a new diet or workout regimen. You also might begin a new project aimed at helping others. With Mars forming a beneficial angle, you can aggressively move ahead with your plans.

Thursday, September 25 (Moon in Libra)   Yesterday's energy related to new opportunities flows into your Thursday. Under the influence of the Libra moon, relationship issues figure prominently, especially involving someone in the workplace. It's also a day for feeding your creative juices. Music, concerts, theaters are highlighted. You're seeking harmony and peace.

Friday, September 26 (Moon into Scorpio, 10:30 a.m.) It's a number 8 day, your power day and your day to play it your way. Open your mind to a new approach, and look for a windfall to come your way. You attract financial success. However, keep in mind that you're playing with power, so be careful not to hurt others.

Saturday, September 27 (Moon in Scorpio)   Mercury moves into your seventh house today, where it stays for a week before going retrograde in Scorpio. There's plenty of emotional interactions with a partner. You attempt to use logic to argue your points, and your mind is quick. There's a tendency to let your feelings interfere with your mind's efforts to remain even tempered.

Sunday, September 28 (Moon into Sagittarius, 6:51 p.m.)   It's a number 1 day. You get a fresh start, a new beginning. Be independent and creative. Don't let others tell you what to do. Get out and meet new people, have new experiences, do something you've never done before. Express your opinions dynamically.

Monday, September 29 (Moon in Sagittarius)   Venus moves into your sixth house today, where it stays until October 23. That means love, happiness, and generosity in the workplace! You feel strongly connected to fellow workers who come to you for help. Do what you can, but know when enough is enough.

Tuesday, September 30 (Moon in Sagittarius) The moon is in your eighth house today. You could be managing another person's money or dealing with an inheritance. Your sense of security or duty is highlighted. Mortgages, taxes, or insurance plays a role in your day. Alternately, you're attracted to the deeper mysteries of life, such as reincarnation or life after death.

OCTOBER 2014

Wednesday, October 1 (Moon into Capricorn, 12:42 a.m.) It's a number 5 day. Promote new ideas; follow your curiosity. Freedom of thought and action is key. It's a good day for a change of scenery. You could be planning a move to a new location. You can overcome obstacles with ease.

Thursday, October 2 (Moon in Capricorn) The moon is in your ninth house today. You're probably feeling restless and looking beyond the everyday scope of your life. Ideas, philosophies, worldviews catch your interest. You could be preparing for or planning a long trip to a foreign country. Alternately, it's a good time to sign up for a workshop or seminar.

Friday, October 3 (Moon into Aquarius, 4:01 a.m.) Stay grounded today, Taurus, and get organized. Persevere to get things done, and don't get sloppy. Tear down the old in order to rebuild. Be methodical and thorough. You're building a creative base for your future. You may feel somewhat inhibited in showing affection now.

Saturday, October 4 (Moon in Aquarius)   Mercury goes retrograde in your seventh house today and stays there until October 25. The energy shifts. You can expect some delays regarding your plans, some disagreements or misunderstandings with a partner. There could be glitches in electronic equipment. You might have to pull the plug and reboot. If you're dealing with a contract, read the fine print carefully before signing. If possible, wait three weeks until Mercury is direct again before signing.

Sunday, October 5 (Moon into Pisces, 5:25 a.m.) It's a number 6 day. Diplomacy wins the way. Be sympathetic and kind, generous and tolerant. Focus on making people happy. Get your new year's resolutions in order; include wishes for others as well as goals for yourself.

Monday, October 6 (Moon in Pisces)   The moon is in your eleventh house today. Friendships are important to you. You could join a group of like-minded people to pursue a project, especially one in which social awareness plays a role. You work for the common good, but keep an eye on your own wishes and dreams.

Tuesday, October 7 (Moon into Aries, 6:07 a.m.) It's your power day, Taurus. Business and financial matters go well. Money comes your way. You intuitively know what decisions to make that will provide you with the greatest income. At least for the day, you are a master of the material world.

Wednesday, October 8 (Moon in Aries) There's a lunar eclipse in your twelfth house today. That means you have an emotional reaction to an event that relates to your past. With Uranus forming a close angle, whatever this event is, it comes suddenly and without warning. Think carefully before you act. Consider: Is it kind, is it true, is it necessary? If you're not careful, there's a tendency now to undo all the positive actions you've taken. You might feel a need to withdraw. Take time to reflect and meditate.

Thursday, October 9 (Moon into Taurus, 7:44 a.m.) It's a number 1 day. You're at the top of your cycle. You can take the lead in a new project. You get a fresh start now, a new beginning. Stress originality. In romance something new is developing. A flirtation could turn serious. Get out and meet new people; have new experiences. Do something you've never done before.

Friday, October 10 (Moon in Taurus) The moon is on your ascendant today. The way you see yourself is the way others see you. You're recharged for the rest of the month, and this makes you more appealing to the public. You're physically vital, and relations with the opposite sex go well.

Saturday, October 11 (Moon into Gemini, 11:51 a.m.) It's a number 3 day. Your charm and wit are appreciated today. Your imagination is keen now, and you communicate well. You're warm and receptive to what others say. Your popularity is definitely on the rise.

Sunday, October 12 (Moon in Gemini)   Yesterday's energy flows into your Sunday. Have a party, socialize, get out and have fun; flirt. A change of scenery works to your benefit. Your mind moves quickly now from one thought to another. You can come up with new money-making ideas.

Monday, October 13 (Moon into Cancer, 7:31 p.m.) Approach the day with an unconventional mindset, Taurus. Change and variety are highlighted. Promote new ideas; follow your curiosity. Think freedom, no restrictions. Take risks; experiment. However, maintain your native common sense and down-to-earth perspective on life.

Tuesday, October 14 (Moon in Cancer)   The moon is in your third house today. You're dealing with your everyday world now, but you're thinking about the big picture. You get your ideas across, but you could be overly influenced by past events. Stay in control of your emotions when talking with others, especially family members.

Wednesday, October 15 (Moon in Cancer)   Under the influence of the Cancer moon, you could be feeling moody today and sensitive to other people's moods. You can be touchy and tend to avoid direct confrontations. You can also be somewhat manipulative, but in your own down-to-earth way. Cancer, Scorpio, and Pisces people play a role.

Thursday, October 16 (Moon into Leo, 6:30 a.m.)
It's another power day, Taurus. Your persistence pays
off. Unexpected money arrives. Business dealings and
finances turn favorable. People in power are watching.
Open your mind to a new approach that could bring
in big bucks.

Friday, October 17 (Moon in Leo)   The moon is
in your fourth house today. It's a good day to beautify
your home; work on a home-repair project. Tend to
your loved ones, but take time to relax and meditate.
You could be dealing with your parents now. You feel
a close tie to your roots.

Saturday, October 18 (Moon into Virgo, 7:09 p.m.)
It's a number 1 day, and so you're at the top of your
cycle again. You get a new beginning, a fresh start.
Take the lead in a new project, and don't be afraid to
turn in a new direction. You're inventive and make
connections that others overlook. You're determined
and courageous today. Stress originality.

Sunday, October 19 (Moon in Virgo)   The moon
is in your fifth house today. Your emotions tend to
overpower your intellect, but you're in touch with
your creative side. You also might be more possessive
of loved ones and protective of children. Animals play
a larger role than usual.

Monday, October 20 (Moon in Virgo)   Under the
influence of the Virgo moon, you feel an urge to exercise and watch your diet, Taurus. Take care of details
now, especially related to your health. Stop worrying

and fretting. Take time to write in a journal. You write from a deep place with lots of details and colorful descriptions.

Tuesday, October 21 (Moon into Libra, 7:13 a.m.) It's a number 4 day. Focus on getting things done today, Taurus, even though you might feel like wandering off task and enjoying the outdoors. Tear down the old in order to rebuild. Use your native persistence. You're building a creative base for your future. Be methodical and thorough. Missing papers or objects are found.

Wednesday, October 22 (Moon in Libra) With the moon in your sixth house today, the emphasis turns to your daily work and service to others. Attend to details, and be careful not to overlook any seemingly minor matters that could take on importance. Keep up with your exercise plan, and watch your diet.

Thursday, October 23 (Moon into Scorpio, 5:11 p.m.) Venus moves into your seventh house today, and there's also a new moon in Scorpio. Opportunities for creative projects abound now, especially ones that involve a partner. You could be getting a contract for such projects. Feelings are heightened, and passions run high for you and your partner.

Friday, October 24 (Moon in Scorpio) Under the influence of the Scorpio moon, yesterday's energy flows into your Friday. Your emotions grow intense as you investigate an important matter. Control issues arise. Be aware of things happening in secret. Forgive and forget; try to avoid going to extremes. You're also passionate today, and your sexuality is heightened.

Saturday, October 25 (Moon in Scorpio) Mercury goes direct today in your sixth house. The delays and misunderstandings are over, Taurus, especially in the workplace. Now you are understood when you're offering your assistance to others. Misunderstandings are resolved. So are the computer glitches.

Sunday, October 26 (Moon into Sagittarius, 12:41 a.m.) Mars moves into your ninth house today. Your mind is active, and you're open to new ideas, new philosophies. You're energetic and determined to pursue higher education or travel to a foreign land. But you don't have much tolerance for those who think you're moving too fast.

Monday, October 27 (Moon in Sagittarius) The moon is in your eighth house today. You could be feeling vulnerable about your partner's income or lack of it. Issues about taxes, a mortgage, or insurance arise. It's an excellent time to have a living will drawn up. You might also take an interest in exploring the larger mysteries, i.e., life after death, past and future lives.

Tuesday, October 28 (Moon into Capricorn, 6:04 a.m.) It's a number 2 day, and that means partnerships take on more importance. Your spouse or partner is at your side. Don't make waves or show resentment, but take time to consider the direction you're headed and your motivation for continuing on this path. Your intuition focuses on relationships.

Wednesday, October 29 (Moon in Capricorn) The moon is in your ninth house today, the home of higher learning. You're full of ideas now on matters such as philosophy or religion, the law or publishing. You also have a strong interest in foreign travel or a foreign nation. It's a good time to look to the big picture. Break away from your routine or the usual way you think about things.

Thursday, October 30 (Moon into Aquarius, 9:52 a.m.) It's a number 4 day. Your organizational skills are highlighted. Control your impulses. Set aside romantic notions for the time being. Persevere, and fulfill your obligations. You're building foundations for your creativity. Emphasize quality.

Friday, October 31 (Moon in Aquarius) The moon is in your tenth house today. It's a good day for gaining recognition. You're in the public eye now. You get along well with fellow workers and are much admired. You have a strong desire for high achievement through hard work, and others respect your efforts.

NOVEMBER 2014

Saturday, November 1 (Moon in Pisces) The moon is in your eleventh house today. You have deeper contact with friends and could join a group of like-minded individuals. Social consciousness plays a role. You work for the common good, but keep an eye on your own wishes and dreams.

Sunday, November 2 —Daylight Saving Time Ends (Moon in Pisces) Under the influence of the Pisces moon, ideas are ripe. You can tap deeply into the collective unconscious for inspiration. Your imagination is highlighted. Watch for psychic events and synchronicities. Keep track of your dreams, including your daydreams.

Monday, November 3 (Moon into Aries, 1:54 p.m.)
It's a number 5 day. You're more open and willing to consider change now, Taurus. Approach the day with an unconventional mindset, a new perspective. Take a risk. Promote new ideas; follow your curiosity. Variety is the spice of life.

Tuesday, November 4 (Moon in Aries) The moon is in your twelfth house today. You might feel a need to withdraw and work on your own. You work behind the scenes. Things concerning the past or your childhood play a role. Best to hide your emotions and moodiness. But you might confide in a true friend.

Wednesday, November 5 (Moon into Taurus, 4:34 p.m.) It's your mystery day, Taurus. Secrets, intrigue, confidential information play a role today. You might feel best working on your own. You investigate, analyze, or simply observe what's going on. You quickly come to a conclusion and wonder why others don't see what you see. It's best to hold off on making any final decisions for a couple of days.

Thursday, November 6 (Moon in Taurus) There's a full moon in your first house today. That means you reap what you've sown related to your health and feelings about yourself. You're now glimpsing the person you are becoming. Your emotional self is in the forefront. With Mars and Pluto forming beneficial angles, you're in the driver's seat. In spite of power plays taking place around you, you come out on top.

Friday, November 7 (Moon into Gemini, 8:45 p.m.)
Visualize the future; set your goals, then make them so. Complete a project; clear up odds and ends. Take an inventory on where things are going in your life. It's a good day to make a donation to a worthy cause.

Saturday, November 8 (Moon in Gemini)   Mercury moves into your seventh house today. You express yourself well now, Taurus, as your speaking abilities expand. You make your points and are clearly understood. You work well with others and can arbitrate any disputes that arise. You're also good at promoting your ideas.

Sunday, November 9 (Moon in Gemini)   The moon is in your second house today, and that bodes well for financial matters. Take care of payments, and collect what's owed you. You equate your financial assets with emotional security. Look at your priorities in handling your income. Your values take on new meaning.

Monday, November 10 (Moon into Cancer, 3:39 a.m.)
Your attitude determines everything today. Spread your good news, Taurus. Ease up on routines. Your imagination is keen now. Your intuition is highlighted. Remain flexible. Your charm and wit are appreciated.

Tuesday, November 11 (Moon in Cancer)   The moon is in your third house today. You get your ideas across, Taurus, especially when you're talking to family members, siblings, and neighbors. You could be taking one or more short trips, and possibly talking on your cell phone. Drive carefully, and take time to check up on your mother.

Wednesday, November 12 (Moon into Leo, 1:45 p.m.) It's a number 5 day. Approach the day with an unconventional mindset. Release old structures; get a new point of view. Variety is the spice of life. Think freedom, no restrictions. Change and variety are highlighted now.

Thursday, November 13 (Moon in Leo)   The moon is in your fourth house today. It's a good day to spend time with your family and other loved ones. Stick close to home. You're dealing with the foundations of who you are and who you are becoming. You feel a close tie to your roots. A parent could be involved in your day.

Friday, November 14 (Moon in Leo)   Under the influence of the Leo moon, you're creative and passionate today. Drama is highlighted, perhaps involving children. Romance feels majestic. Dress boldly; showmanship is emphasized.

Saturday, November 15 (Moon into Virgo, 2:09 a.m.) Neptune goes direct in your eleventh house today. You'll become more intuitive in the coming months and also more sensitive. You'll also be more comfortable working with others, especially friends. You start to take a closer look at your wishes and dreams, and fantasy plays a role.

Sunday, November 16 (Moon in Virgo)   Venus moves into your eighth house today. You could have a relationship over the next few weeks with someone whom you've known in a past life. You also could decide now to attend a metaphysical class and explore mysteries of life and death. You could inherit money. Whatever happens, it'll be a positive experience.

Monday, November 17 (Moon into Libra, 2:31 p.m.) It's a number 1 day, so you're at the top of your cycle. It's a great time for initiating new projects, launching new ideas, or brainstorming for new ways of making money. You take the lead on something new as you get a fresh start. Follow your heart.

Tuesday, November 18 (Moon in Libra)   The moon is in your sixth house today. It's a good day to offer your services to others. However, don't deny your own needs. Keep your resolutions about exercise, and watch your diet. Attend to details related to your health.

Wednesday, November 19 (Moon in Libra)   Under the influence of the Libra moon, romance is highlighted. Relationship issues figure prominently in your day. Museums, art, music, creativity all figure in. You're seeking peace and harmony now.

Thursday, November 20 (Moon into Scorpio, 12:32 a.m.)   It's a number 4 day. That means the emphasis today is on your organizational skills. In romance your persistence pays off. You're building a foundation for the future. Be methodical and thorough. Fulfill your obligations. Emphasize quality.

Friday, November 21 (Moon in Scorpio)   The moon is in your seventh house today. You get along well with others now. You can fit in just about anywhere. Loved ones and partners are more important than usual. You comprehend the nuances of a situation, but it's difficult to go with the flow. Be careful that others don't manipulate your feelings.

Saturday, November 22 (Moon into Sagittarius, 7:20 a.m.)   There's a new moon in your eighth house today. That means new opportunities arise now related to joint finances, an inheritance, or investments. You could begin managing someone else's resources. Alternately, you might have a chance to pursue a metaphysical matter, such as getting a past-life reading.

Sunday, November 23 (Moon in Sagittarius)   Under the influence of the Sagittarius moon, you see the big picture. Publishing or the law could play a role. Travel is indicated. There's passion in relationships now. Don't limit yourself. You're restless, impulsive, and inquisitive.

Monday, November 24 (Moon into Capricorn, 11:32 a.m.)   It's your power day, Taurus. You're in the driver's seat. Business dealings go your way. You attract financial success. Think big and act big! People in power are watching.

Tuesday, November 25 (Moon in Capricorn) The moon is in your ninth house today. You may feel a need to get away now, a need to grow and expand your horizons, a break from the usual routine. You yearn for a new experience. Foreigners or a foreign country plays a role in your day. It's a good time to plan a long trip or sign up for a workshop or seminar.

Wednesday, November 26 (Moon into Aquarius, 2:23 p.m.) You get a fresh start, a new beginning. You can take the lead now, and don't be afraid to turn in a new direction. Trust your hunches; intuition is highlighted. You're inventive and make connections that others overlook. You're determined and courageous today.

Thursday, November 27 (Moon in Aquarius) Mercury moves into your eighth house today. Expect lots of discussions with a partner about mortgages, insurance, and investments. You also could be dealing with a metaphysical matter and talking with someone close to you about ghosts or life after death. You're looking for answers and exchanging ideas with others.

Friday, November 28 (Moon into Pisces, 5:04 p.m.) You can influence people now with your upbeat attitude. Your charm and wit are appreciated. Your attitude determines everything today. Spread your good news. Ease up on routines, and remain flexible.

Saturday, November 29 (Moon in Pisces) The moon is in your eleventh house today. Friends play an important role in your day, especially Capricorn and Virgo. You're grounded, Taurus, and work well with a group, but don't overlook your own goals. Focus on your wishes and dreams, and make sure that they remain an expression of who you are.

Sunday, November 30 (Moon into Aries, 8:15 p.m.)
Freedom of thought and action is highlighted. So is moderation in all that you do, Taurus. A change of scenery would work to your advantage. You could be moving to a new location. Think outside the box. It's a good day to take a risk. Promote new ideas; follow your curiosity. Look for adventure.

DECEMBER 2014

Monday, December 1 (Moon in Aries)   The moon is in your twelfth house today. Think carefully before you act. There's a tendency now to undo all the positive actions you've taken. Avoid any self-destructive behavior. Caution is the key word of the day. It's best to work behind the scenes. Be aware of secret enemies. Take time to reflect and meditate.

Tuesday, December 2 (Moon in Aries)   Under the influence of the Aries moon, you're feeling passionate but impatient today. You're extremely persuasive now, especially if you're passionate about what you're doing, selling, or trying to convey. Imprint your style; wear bright colors. It's a good day to attend a sports event.

Wednesday, December 3 (Moon into Taurus, 12:16 a.m.)   It's a number 6 day, a service day. Be understanding, and avoid confrontations. Diplomacy wins the way. Focus on making people happy, but avoid scattering your energies. Be sympathetic, kind, and compassionate.

Thursday, December 4 (Moon in Taurus) Mars moves into your tenth house today, where it stays until January 12. Expect plenty of activity with coworkers over the coming weeks. You let others know that you deserve a raise or promotion, at least a boost in prestige. Control your aggressiveness, and coworkers will support your efforts.

Friday, December 5 (Moon into Gemini, 5:29 a.m.) It's a number 8 day, your power day and your day to play it your way. You can go far with your plans to achieve financial success. You have a chance to expand, to gain recognition, even fame and power.

Saturday, December 6 (Moon in Gemini) There's a full moon in your second house of money today, and that means you gain insight related to finances or your values. Meanwhile, Uranus forms a beneficial angle, suggesting that unexpected events related to money matters work to your benefit. Your mind is sharp, and with Jupiter in your favor now you can expand whatever you're doing. Look to the big picture as well as the past.

Sunday, December 7 (Moon into Cancer, 12:35 p.m.) You're at the top of your cycle again, Taurus. Stress originality in whatever you're doing. Don't fear change. Explore, discover, create. Express your opinions dynamically, but refuse to deal with people who have closed minds. You attract creative people.

Monday, December 8 (Moon in Cancer) Jupiter goes retrograde in your fourth house today and stays that way until April 8. You could face some delays in plans to renovate or sell your home. Whatever you're dealing with in your home may take longer than you think. Meanwhile, any plans to buy a new house could be put on hold.

Tuesday, December 9 (Moon into Leo, 10:15 p.m.) Your charm and wit are appreciated today. Your imagination is keen, and you communicate well. You're warm and receptive to what others say. Your popularity is definitely on the rise. Relax, enjoy yourself, recharge your batteries.

Wednesday, December 10 (Moon in Leo) Venus moves into your ninth house today, where it stays until January 4. You have a love of travel and philosophy and are exercising your intellect as you learn more about the world. You appreciate the finer things in life. The next three weeks are a good time to plan a long journey, and you're especially intuitive about details.

Thursday, December 11 (Moon in Leo) The moon is in your fourth house. You're dealing with foundations now, the very foundations of who you are and who you are becoming. Make an effort to change a bad habit. It's best today to work on your own. Spend time with your family and other loved ones; work on a project to beautify your home.

Friday, December 12 (Moon into Virgo, 10:20 a.m.) It's another service day, Taurus. You offer advice and support. Focus on making people happy. Be sympathetic, kind, and compassionate. A domestic adjustment works out for the best. Diplomacy wins the way.

Saturday, December 13 (Moon in Virgo) The moon is in your fifth house today. Be yourself; be emotionally honest. There's greater emotional depth in a relationship now. You're emotionally in touch with your creative side. In fact, your emotions tend to overpower your intellect. You're more protective and nurturing toward children.

Sunday, December 14 (Moon into Libra, 11:05 p.m.) It's a number 8 day, your power day. Open your mind to a new approach. Unexpected resources arrive. You can go far with your plans and achieve financial success. But be aware that you're playing with power, so try not to hurt anyone.

Monday, December 15 (Moon in Libra) The moon is in your sixth house today. It's a service day. You're the one others go to for help. Offer assistance, but don't deny your own needs. It's best if you follow a regular schedule now. It's a good day to clarify any health or work issues. Visit someone who is sick.

Tuesday, December 16 (Moon in Libra) Mercury moves into your ninth house today, where it stays until January 5. You're seriously discussing your thoughts about pursuing higher education or taking a workshop or seminar. You take an interest in philosophy, mythology, the law, publishing, or other fields. It's a good time to explore plans for foreign travel.

Wednesday, December 17 (Moon into Scorpio, 9:52 a.m.)   It's a number 2 day. Help comes through friends. A partner or lover plays a role. Focus on your direction, your motivation. Where are you going and why? The spotlight is on cooperation. Show your appreciation to others.

Thursday, December 18 (Moon in Scorpio)   The moon is in your seventh house today. The focus again is on relationships, personal ones and business alike. You get along well with others, and you fit in just about anywhere. Loved ones and partners are more important than usual. Take time to consider how others see you.

Friday, December 19 (Moon into Sagittarius, 4:56 p.m.)   Your organizational skills are highlighted. Control your impulses; stay focused. Take care of your obligations. You're building foundations for an outlet for your creativity.

Saturday, December 20 (Moon in Sagittarius) The moon is in your eighth house today. You could be dealing with inherited money, also taxes and investments. Whatever it is affects your feelings about shared income or possessions. Control your emotions. You could be dealing with powerful people.

Sunday, December 21 (Moon into Capricorn, 8:26 p.m.)   There's a new moon in your ninth house today. That means the focus is on your education or travel plans, as new opportunities come your way. You might get accepted to a higher-education program or find out about a special deal on tickets to a distant destination. Your interest in philosophy, religion, or mythology is highlighted. Meanwhile, with Uranus going direct in your twelfth house, you could get some upsetting news about someone or something from your past.

Monday, December 22 (Moon in Capricorn) The moon is in your ninth house today. You're a dreamer and thinker. You may feel a need to get away now, a break from the usual routine. You yearn for a new experience. It's a good time to plan a long trip or sign up for a workshop or seminar.

Tuesday, December 23 (Moon into Aquarius, 9:53 p.m.) Saturn enters your eighth house today, where it stays for two and a half years. That means issues could arise over coming months related to income or possessions you share with someone, such as a spouse. You also could face difficulties related to taxes, a mortgage, or credit cards. Keep close tabs on your emotions, especially when talking about financial issues you need to resolve.

Wednesday, December 24 (Moon in Aquarius) The moon is in your tenth house today. Focus on your professional concerns. You could be dealing with bosses and others in power. You can be more responsive to the needs and moods of others around you. You keep everyone around you grounded, Taurus. But make sure you stay grounded yourself. A word of caution: An office romance could be dangerous.

Thursday, December 25 (Moon into Pisces, 11:08 p.m.) It's a number 1 day. You're at the top of your cycle now. Trust your hunches. You're inventive and make connections that others overlook. You're determined and courageous today. As yesterday, be aware that a flirtation could turn serious. Merry Christmas!

Friday, December 26 (Moon in Pisces) The moon is in your eleventh house today. Friends play an important role in your day, especially Virgo and Capricorn. You find strength in numbers. You find meaning through friends and groups, especially a group of like-minded people working for the common good.

Saturday, December 27 (Moon in Pisces) Under the influence of the Pisces moon, your imagination is highlighted. You respond emotionally to whatever is happening now. Keep track of your dreams, including your daydreams. Ideas are ripe. You can tap deeply into the collective unconscious for inspiration. It's a day for deep healing.

Sunday, December 28 (Moon into Aries, 1:36 a.m.) It's a number 4 day. The emphasis today is on your organizational skills. In romance your persistence pays off, especially if you've taken care of all the issues that prevented you from moving ahead with the relationship. You're building a foundation for the future. Take care of obligations, Taurus. You could find missing papers now.

Monday, December 29 (Moon in Aries) The moon is in your twelfth house today. It's a good day to work behind the scenes. You're sensitive now to what others say or do. Think carefully before you act. There's a tendency to undo all the positive actions you've taken. Avoid any self-destructive behavior, and be aware of hidden enemies.

Tuesday, December 30 (Moon into Taurus, 5:57 a.m.)
It's a number 6 day. Do a good deed for someone. Visit someone who is ill or in need of help. Focus on making people happy. Be diplomatic, understanding, and generous with your time.

Wednesday, December 31 (Moon in Taurus) The moon is on your ascendant today. The way you see yourself now is the way others see you. You're recharged for the month ahead, and this makes you more appealing to the public. You're physically vital, and relations with the opposite sex go well. You're sensitive to other people's feelings.

HAPPY NEW YEAR!

SYDNEY OMARR

Born on August 5, 1926, in Philadelphia, Pennsylvania, **Sydney Omarr** was the only person ever given full-time duty in the U.S. Army as an astrologer. He is regarded as the most erudite astrologer of the twentieth century and the best known, through his syndicated column and his radio and television programs (he was Merv Griffin's "resident astrologer"). Omarr has been called the most "knowledgeable astrologer since Evangeline Adams." His forecasts of Nixon's downfall, the end of World War II in mid-August of 1945, the assassination of John F. Kennedy, Roosevelt's election to a fourth term and his death in office . . . these and many others are on the record and quoted enough to be considered "legendary."

ABOUT THE SERIES

This is one of a series of twelve *Sydney Omarr®
Day-by-Day Astrological Guides* for the signs of
2014. For questions and comments about the
book, go to www.sydneyomarr.blogspot.com.